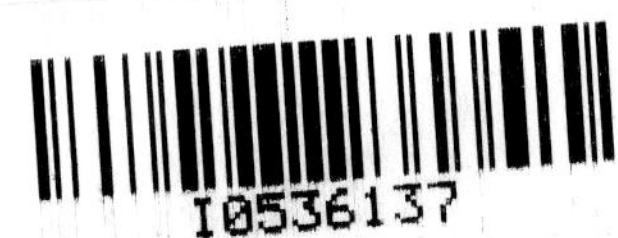

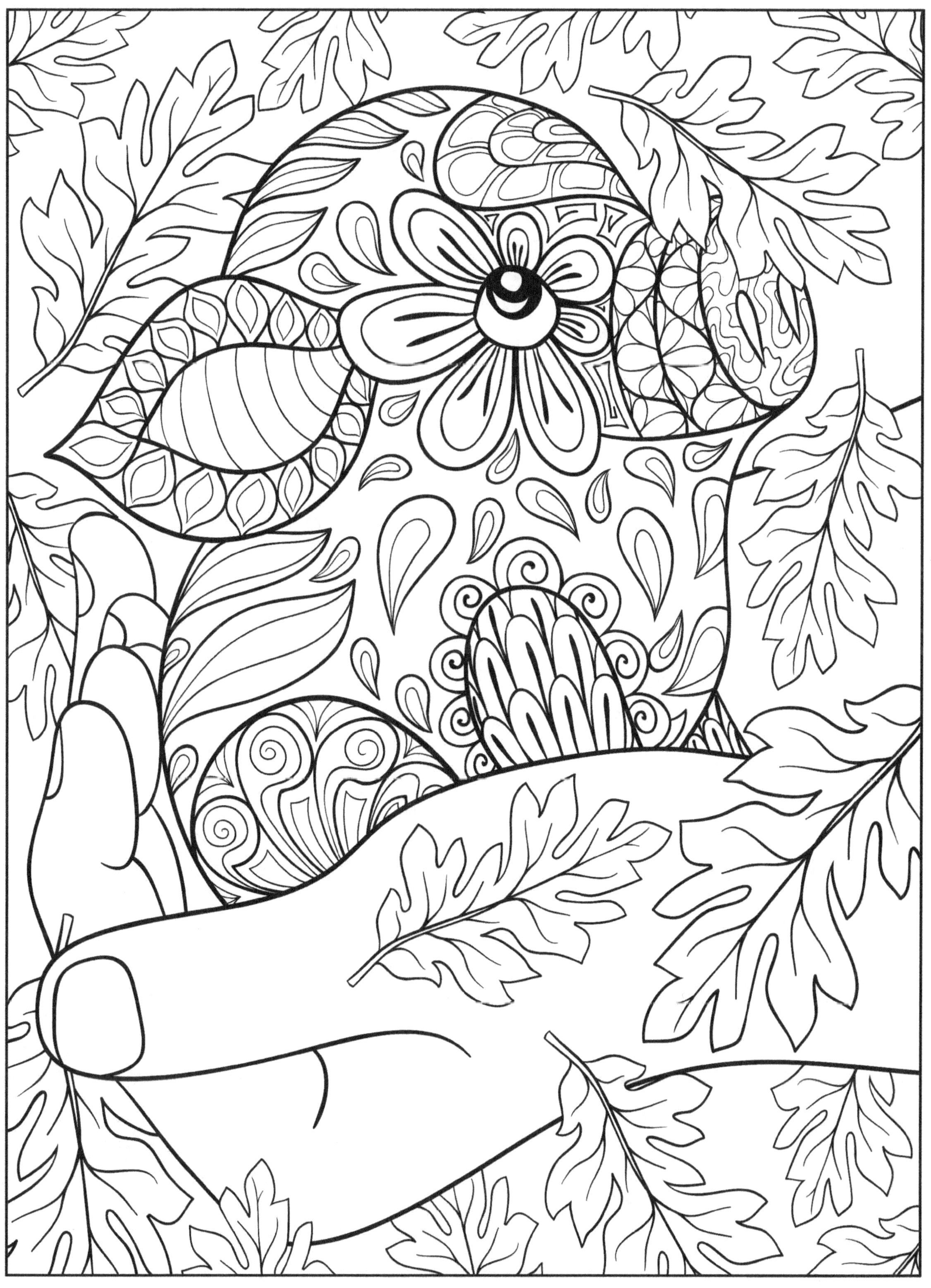

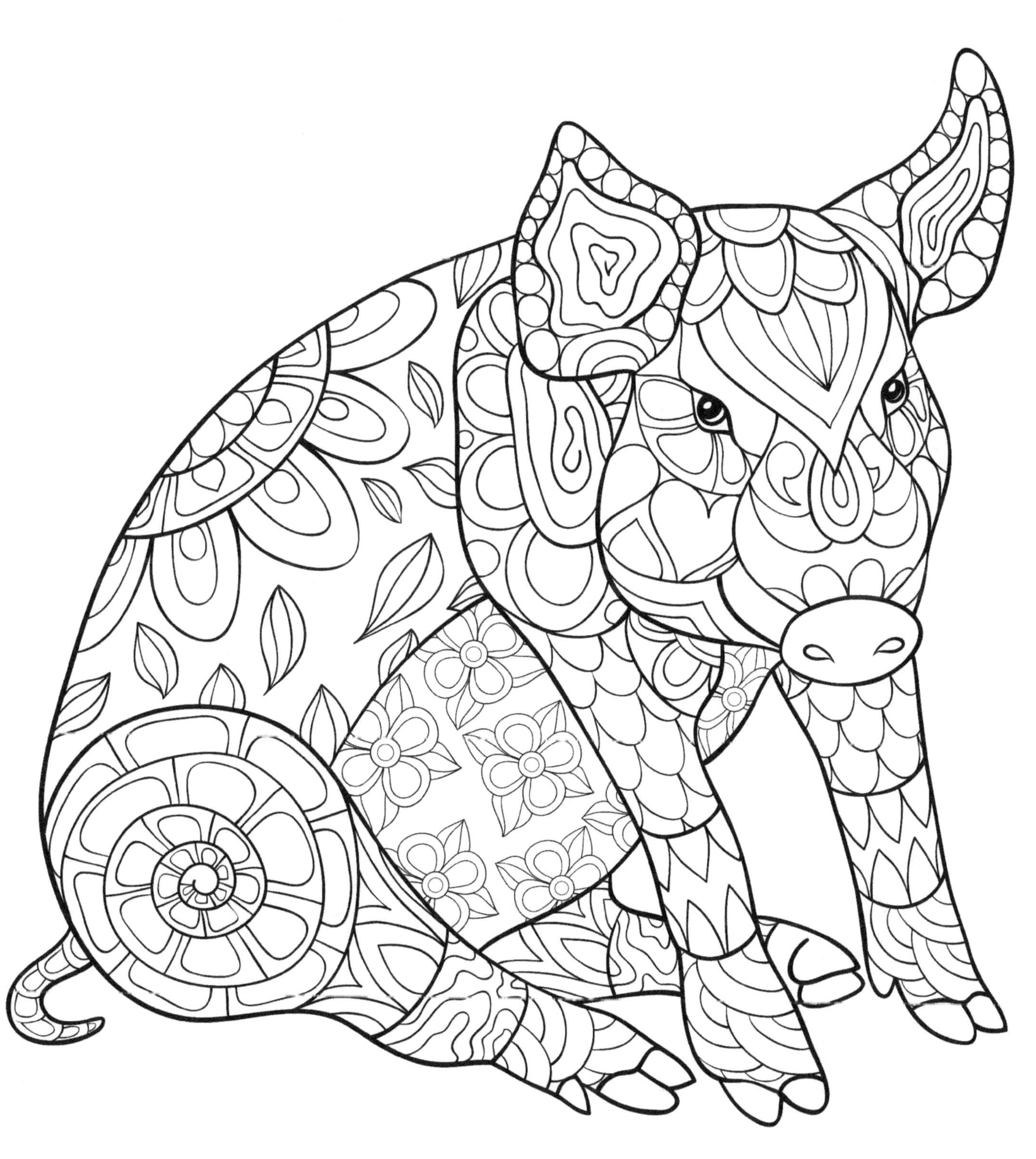

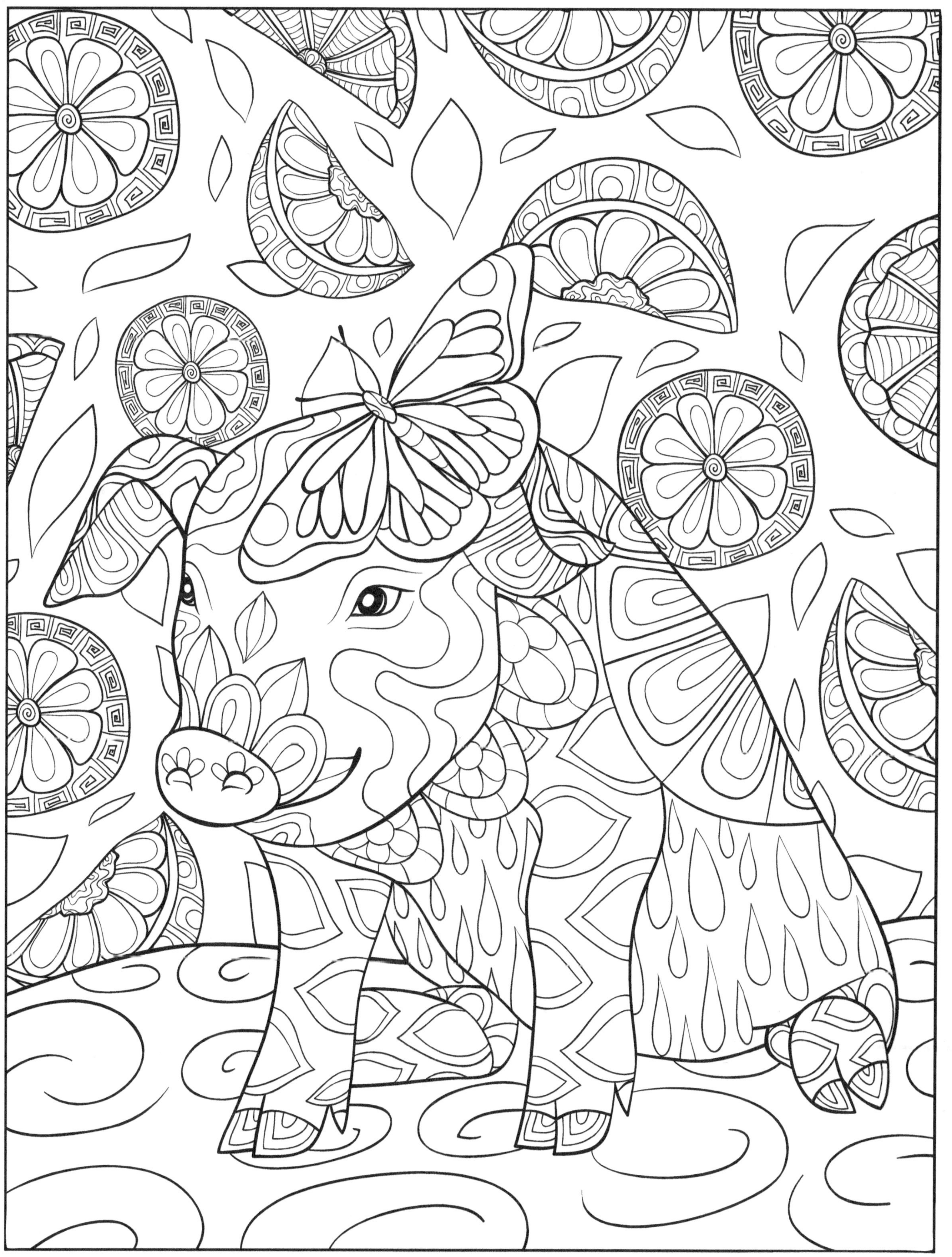

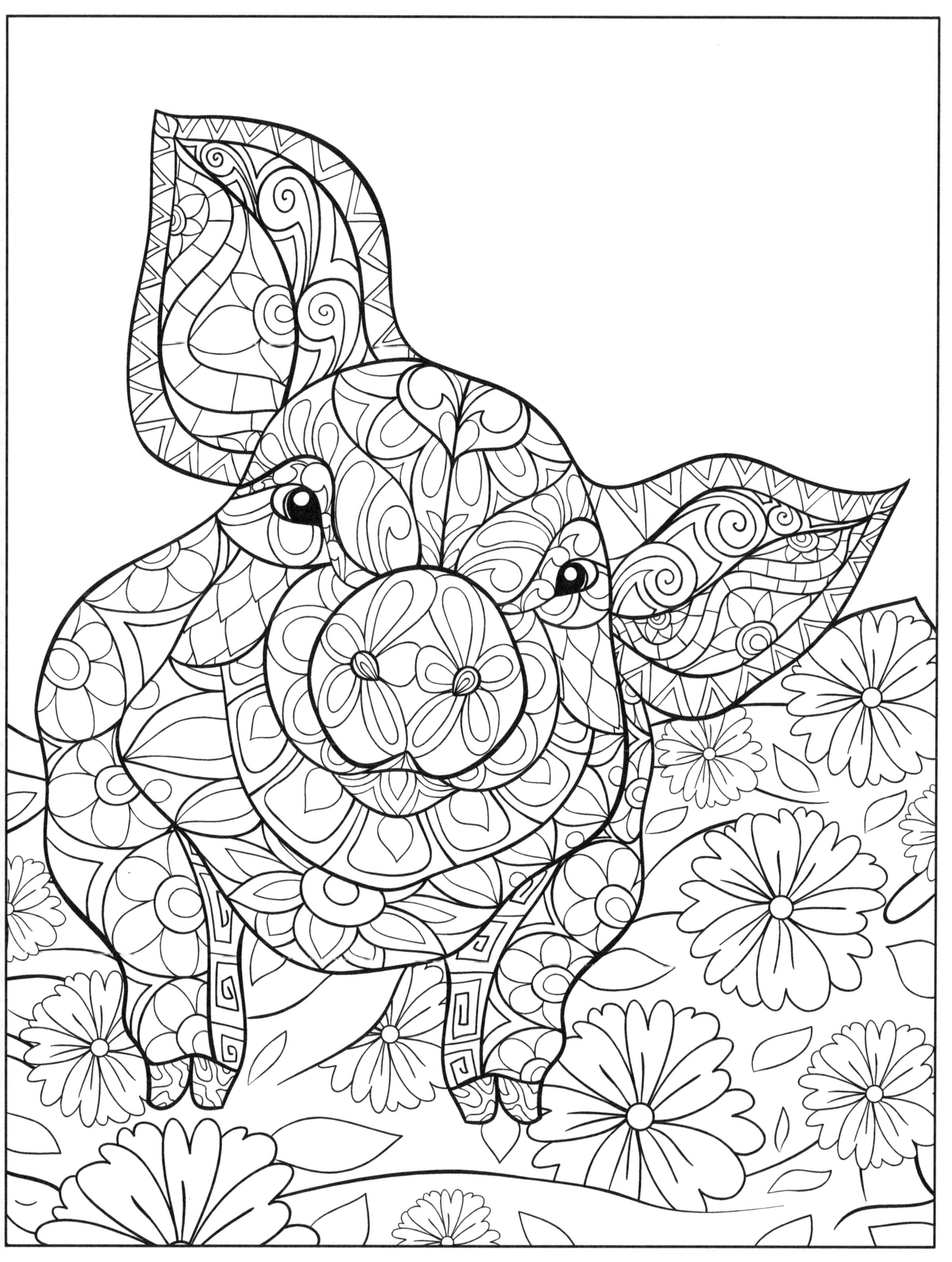

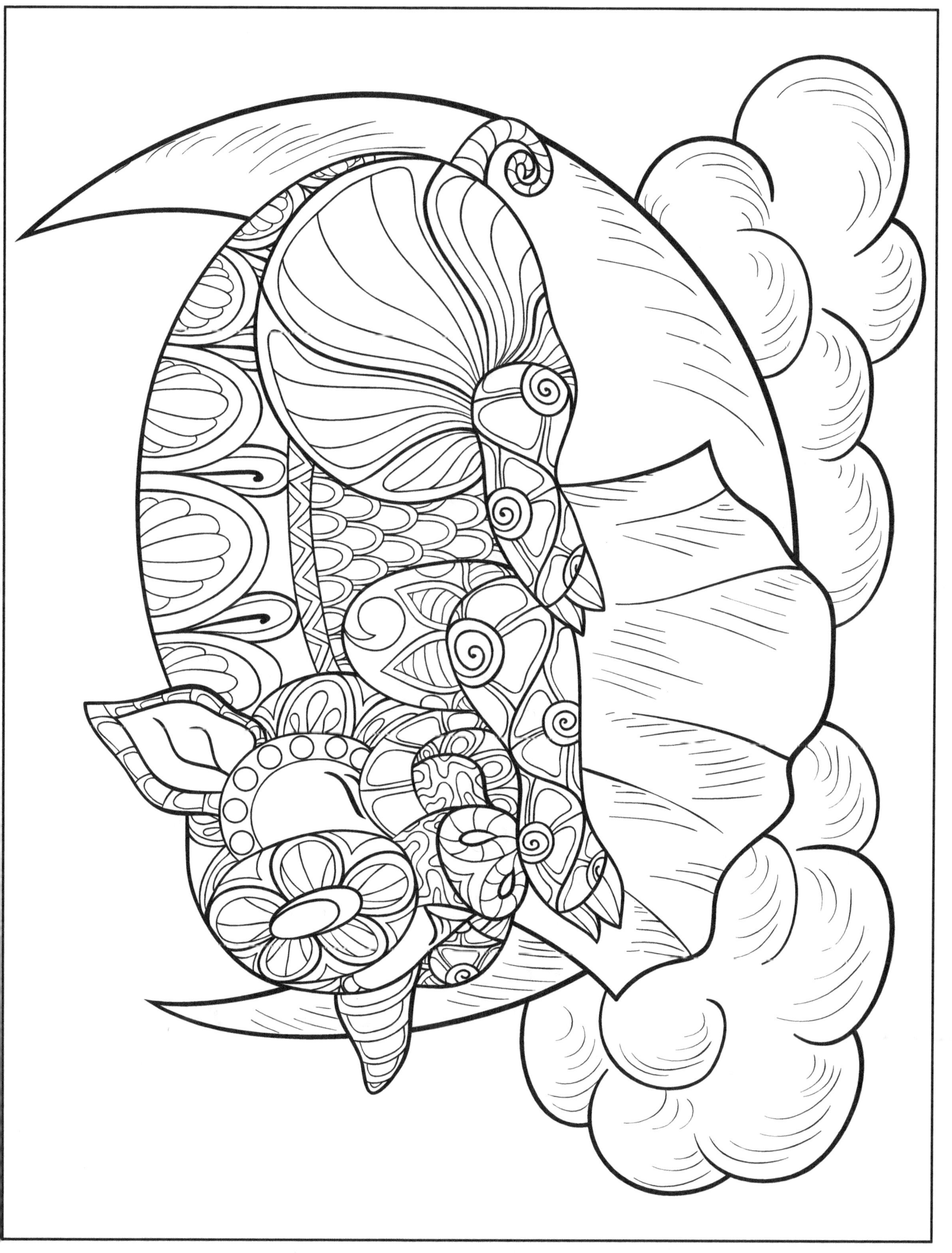

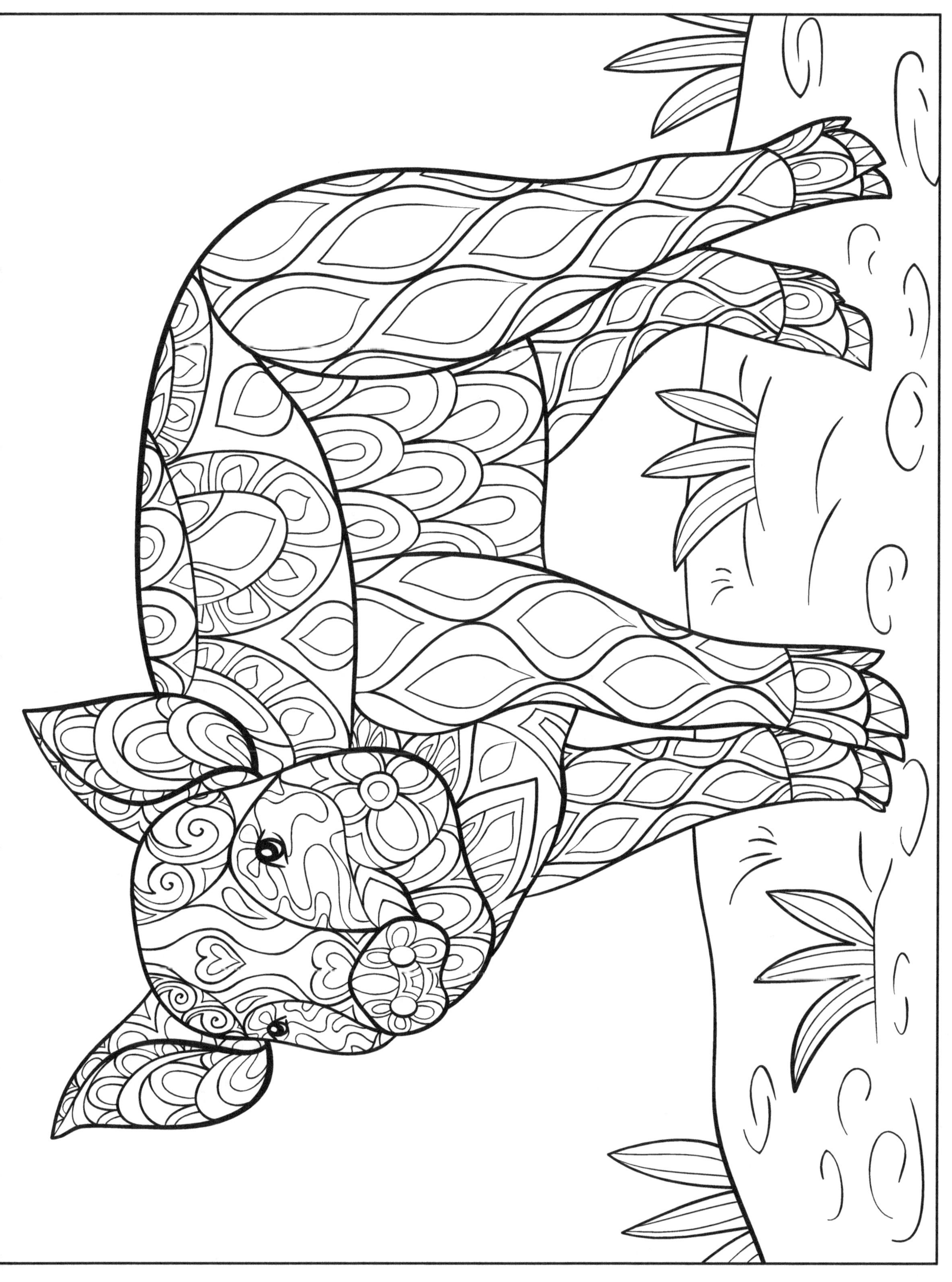

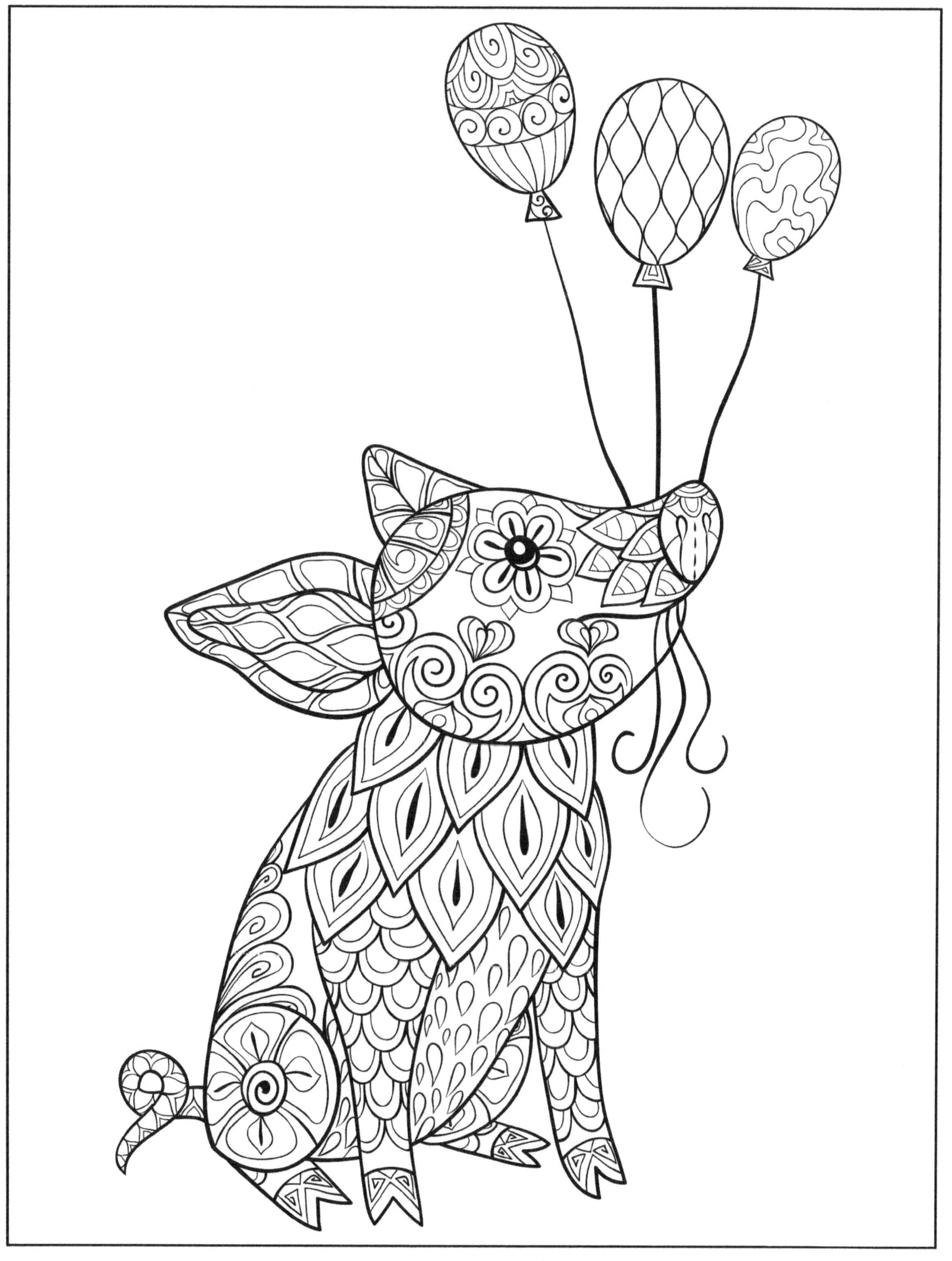

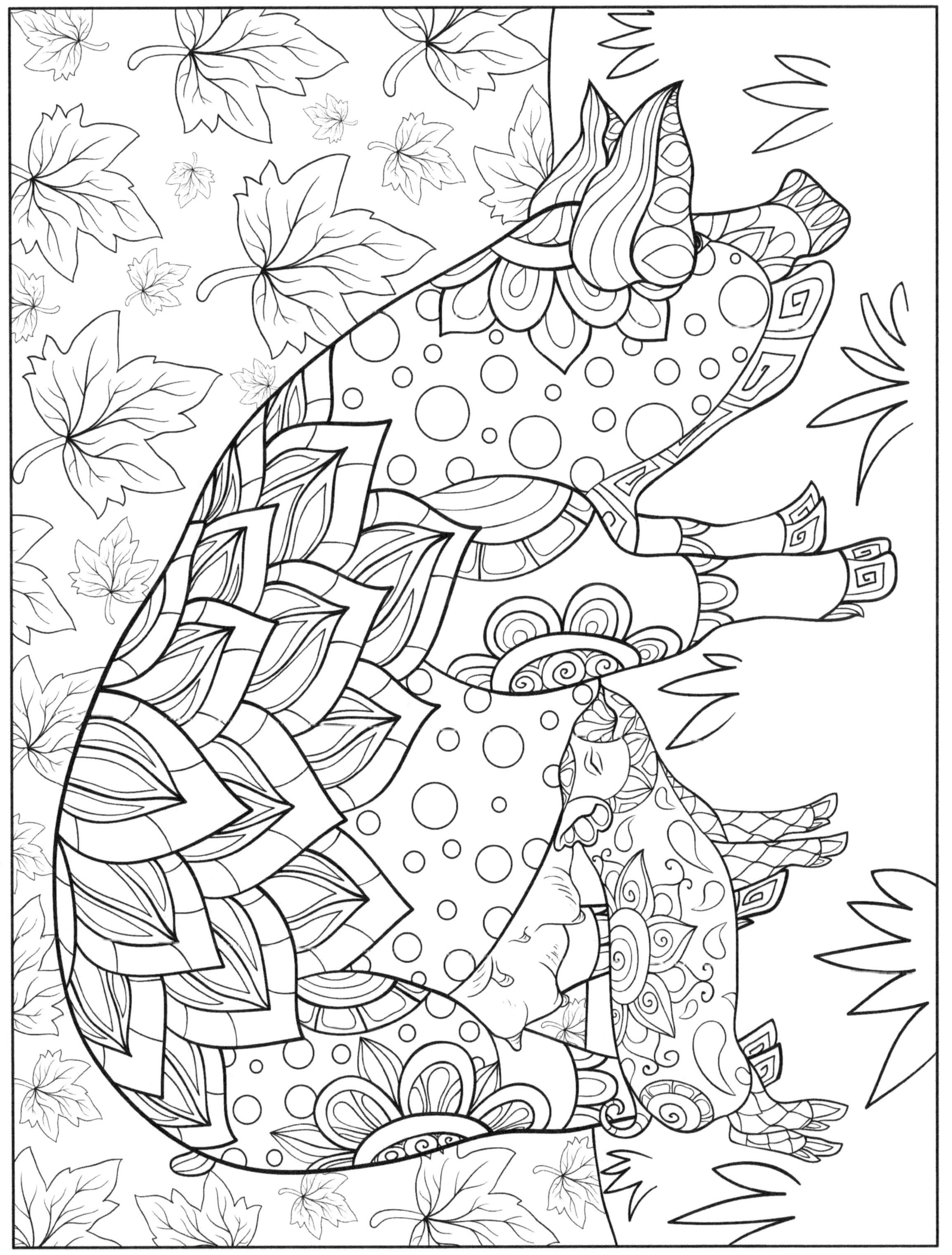

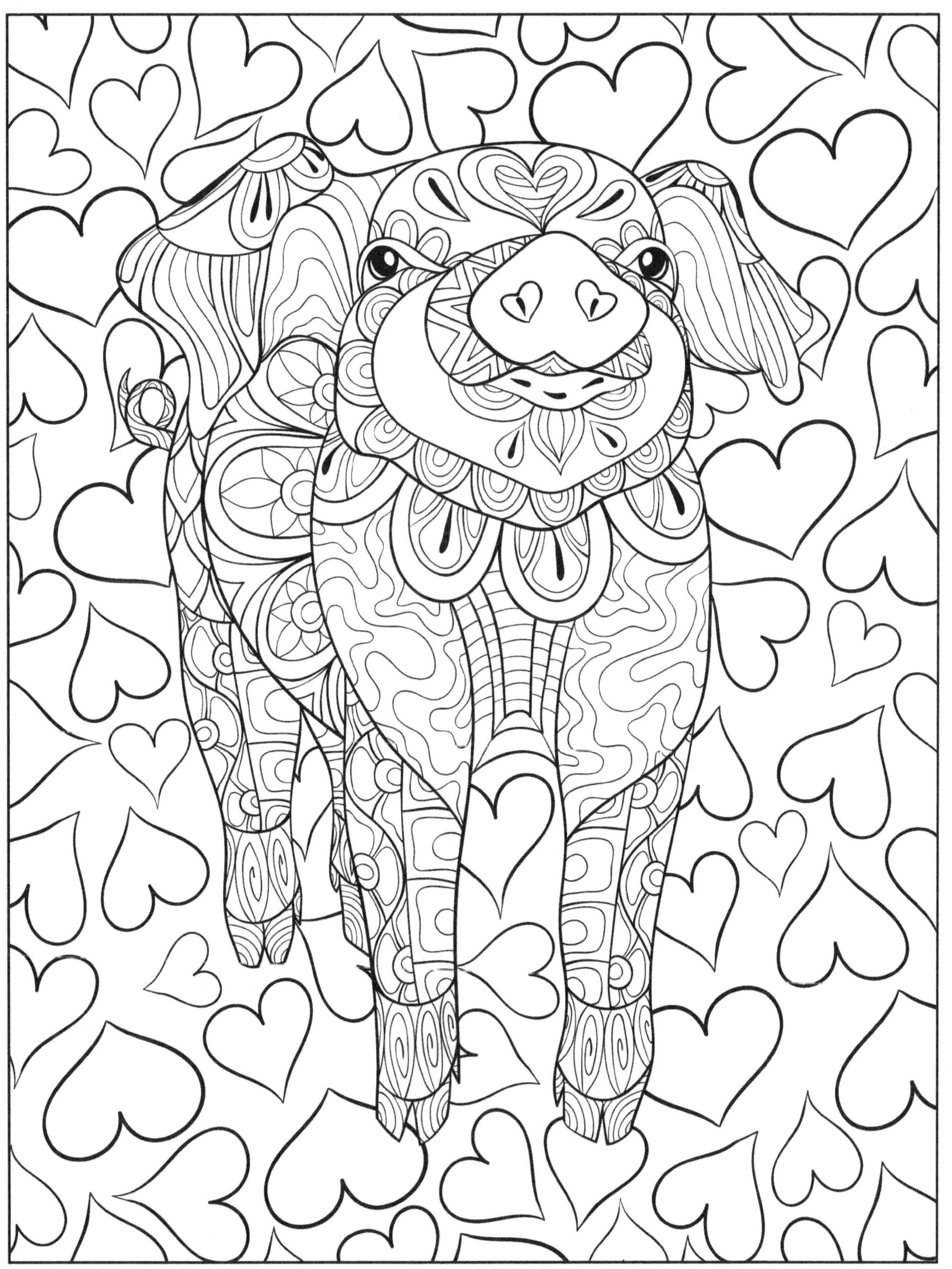

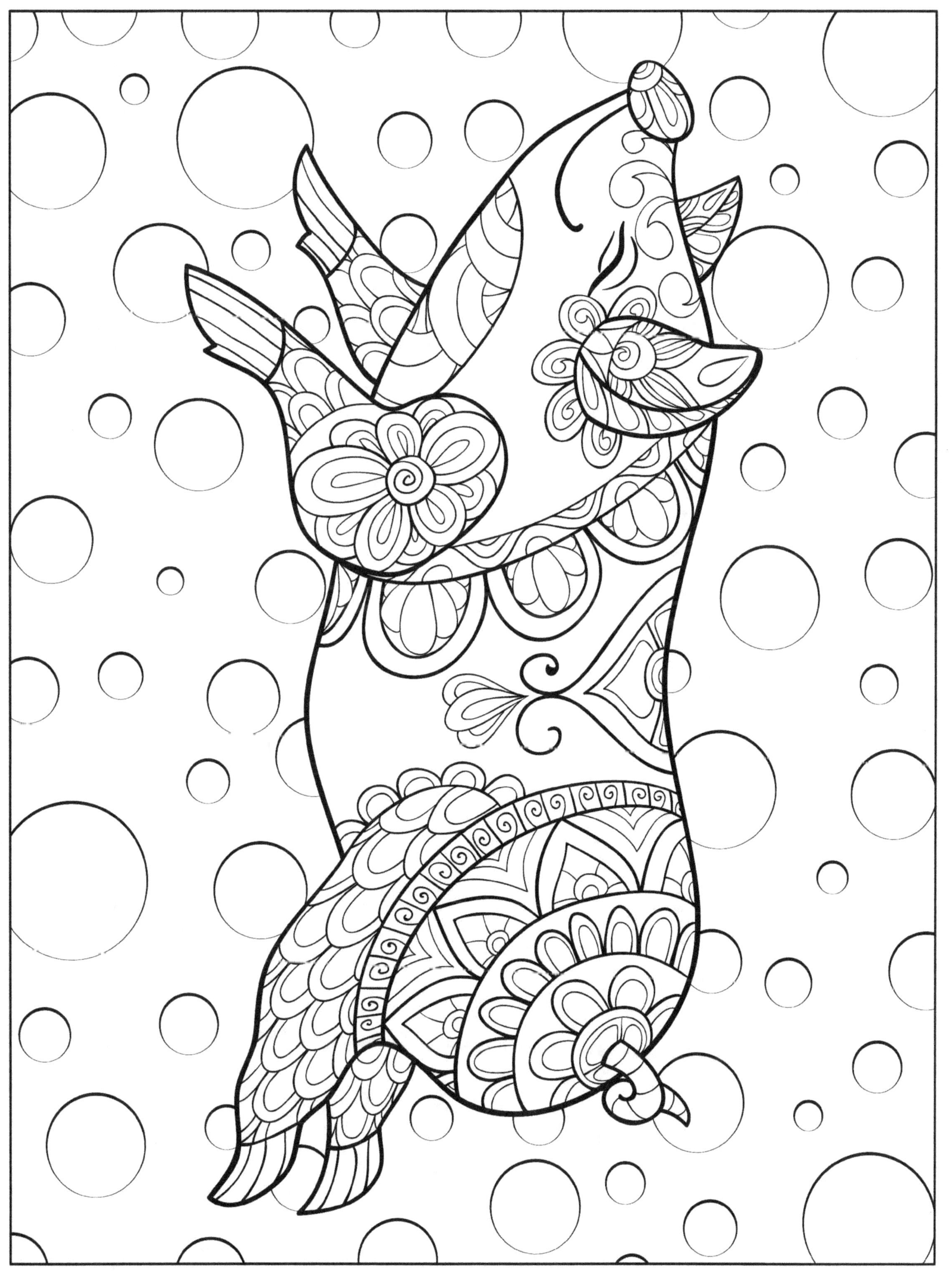

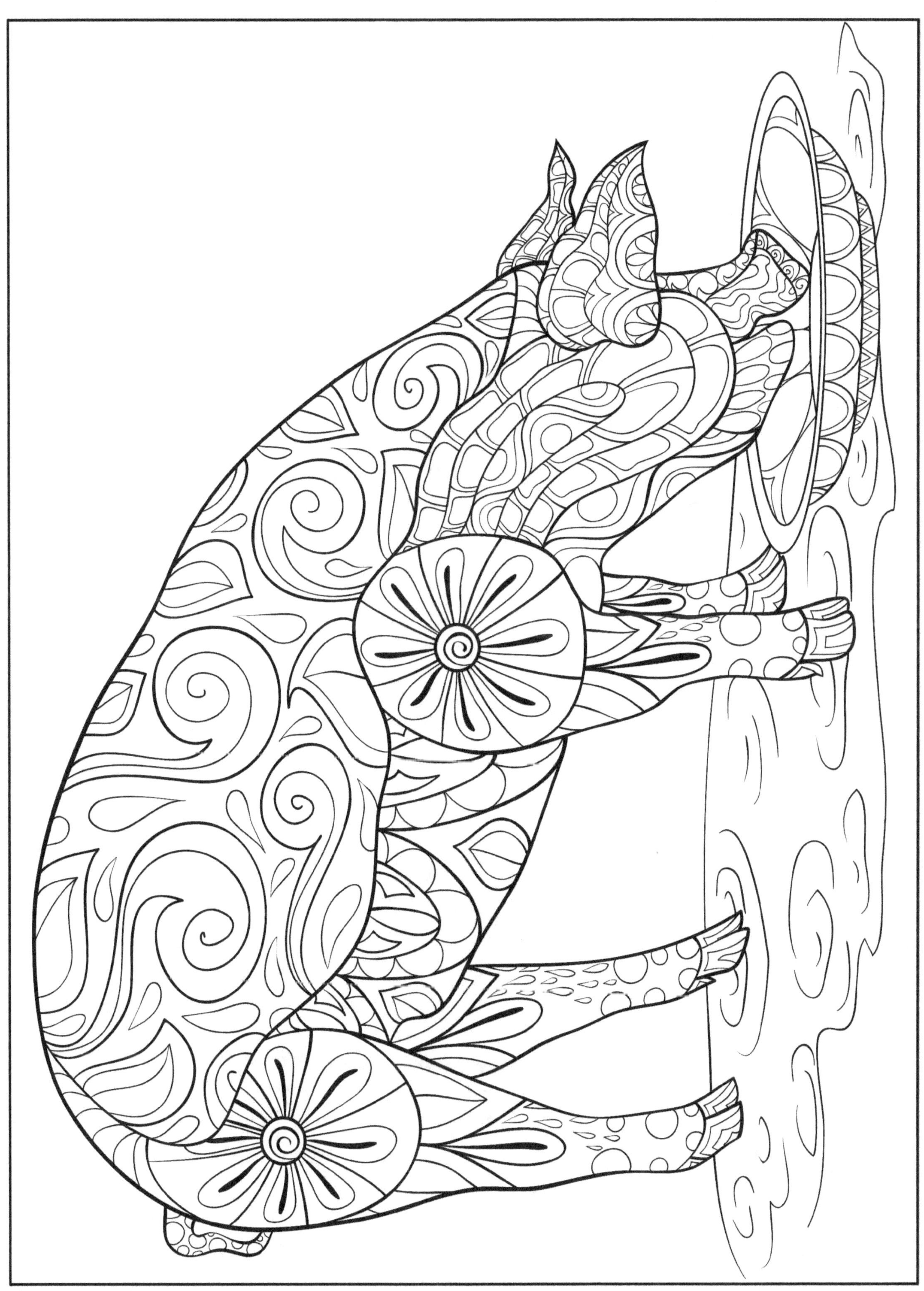

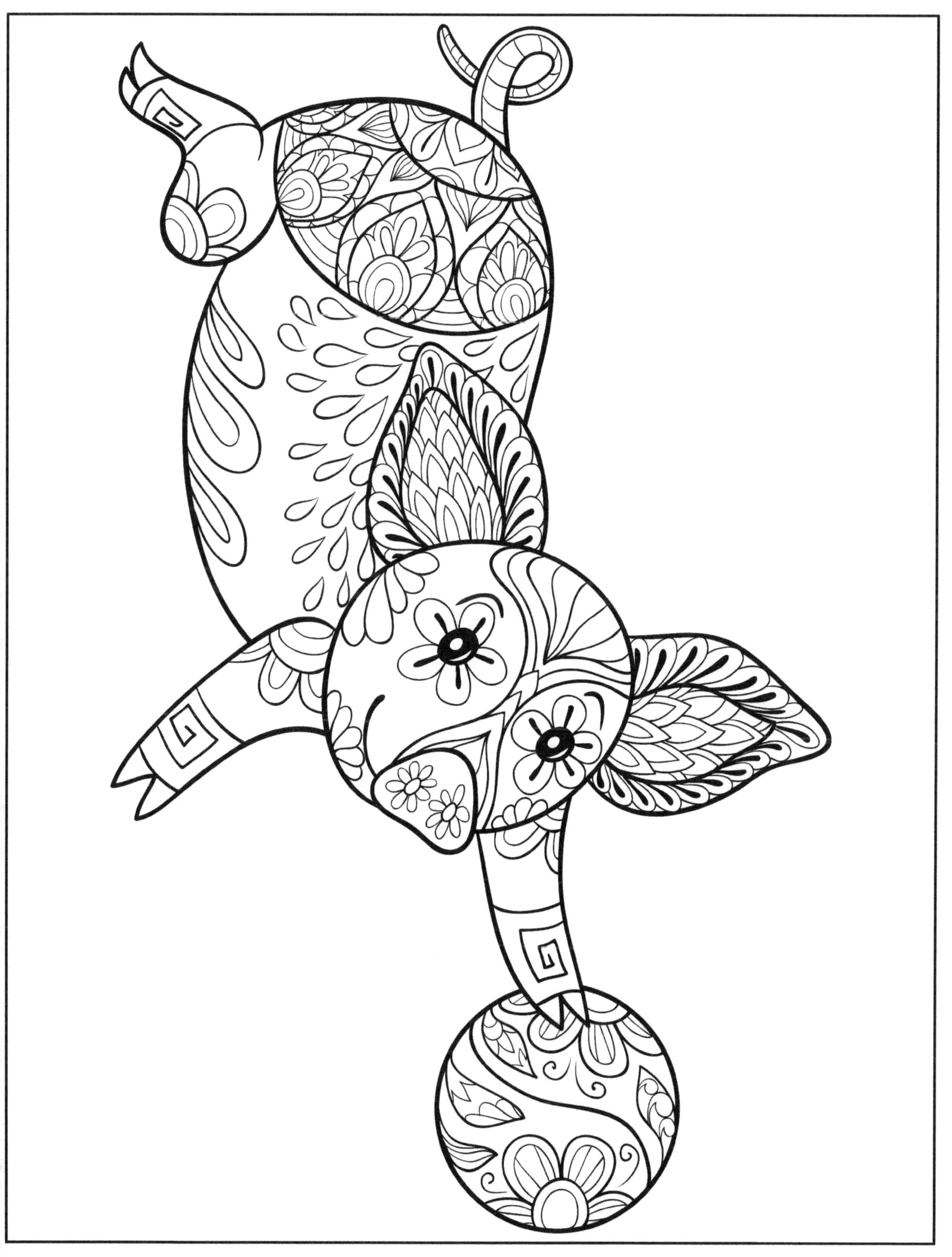

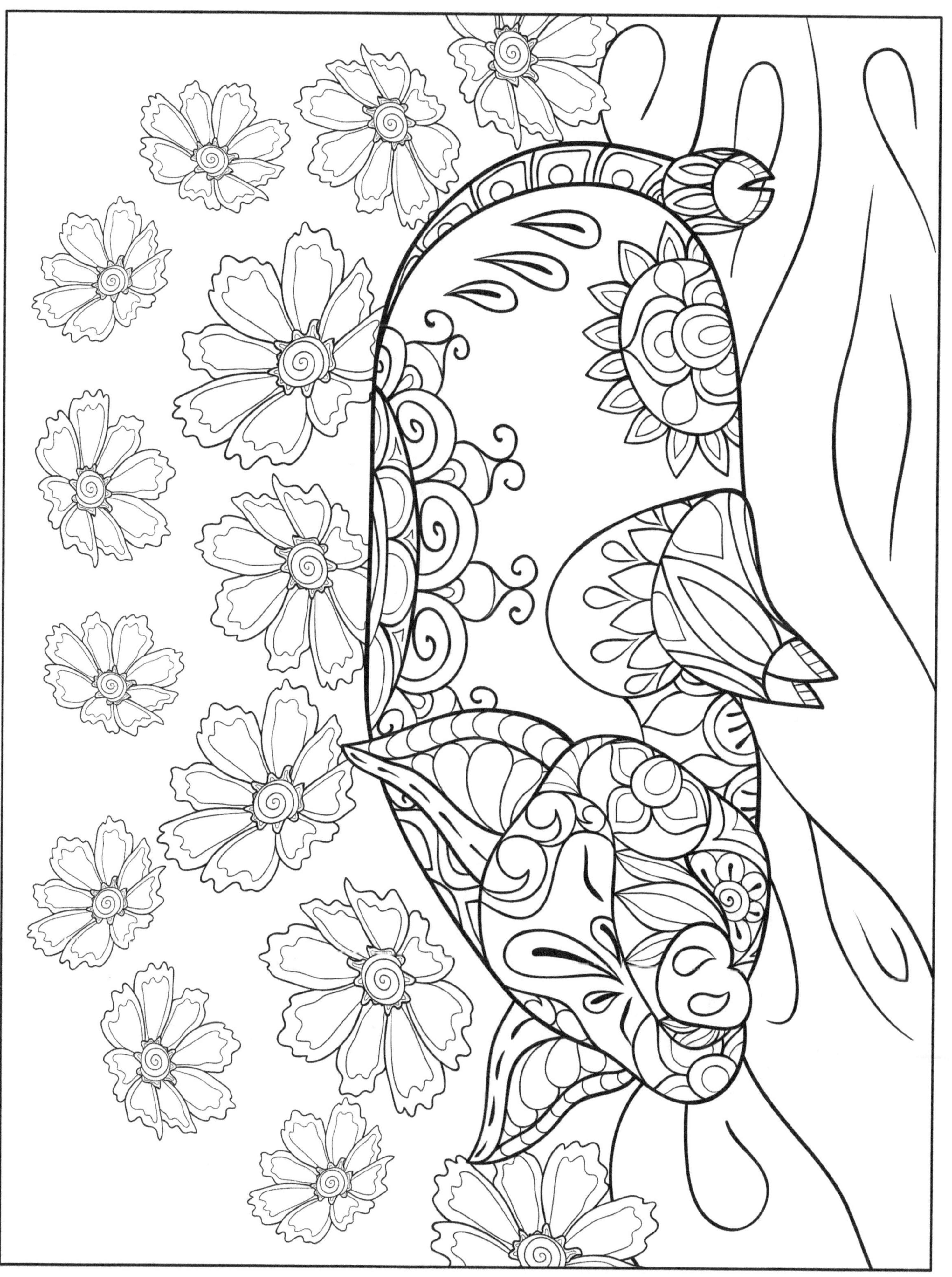

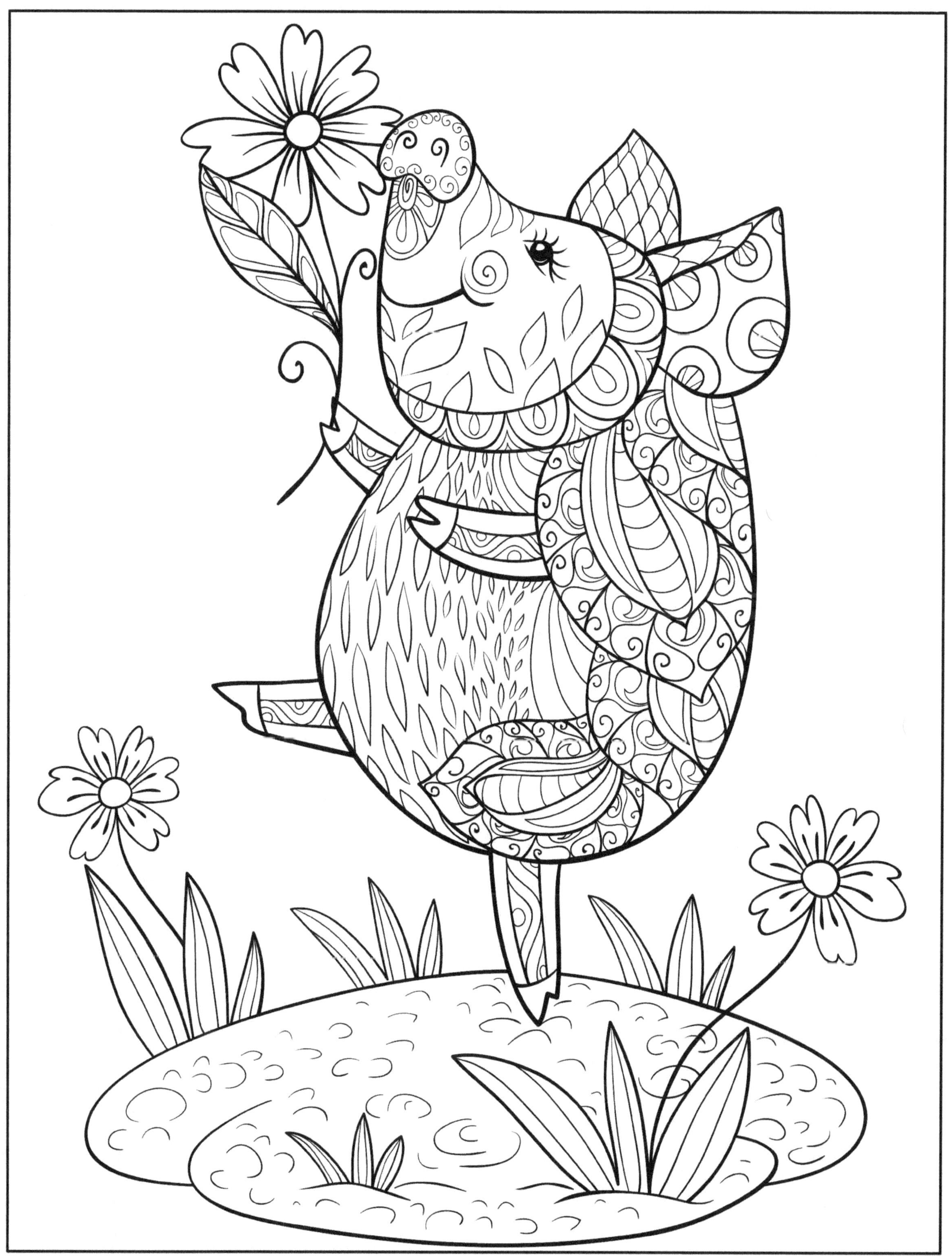

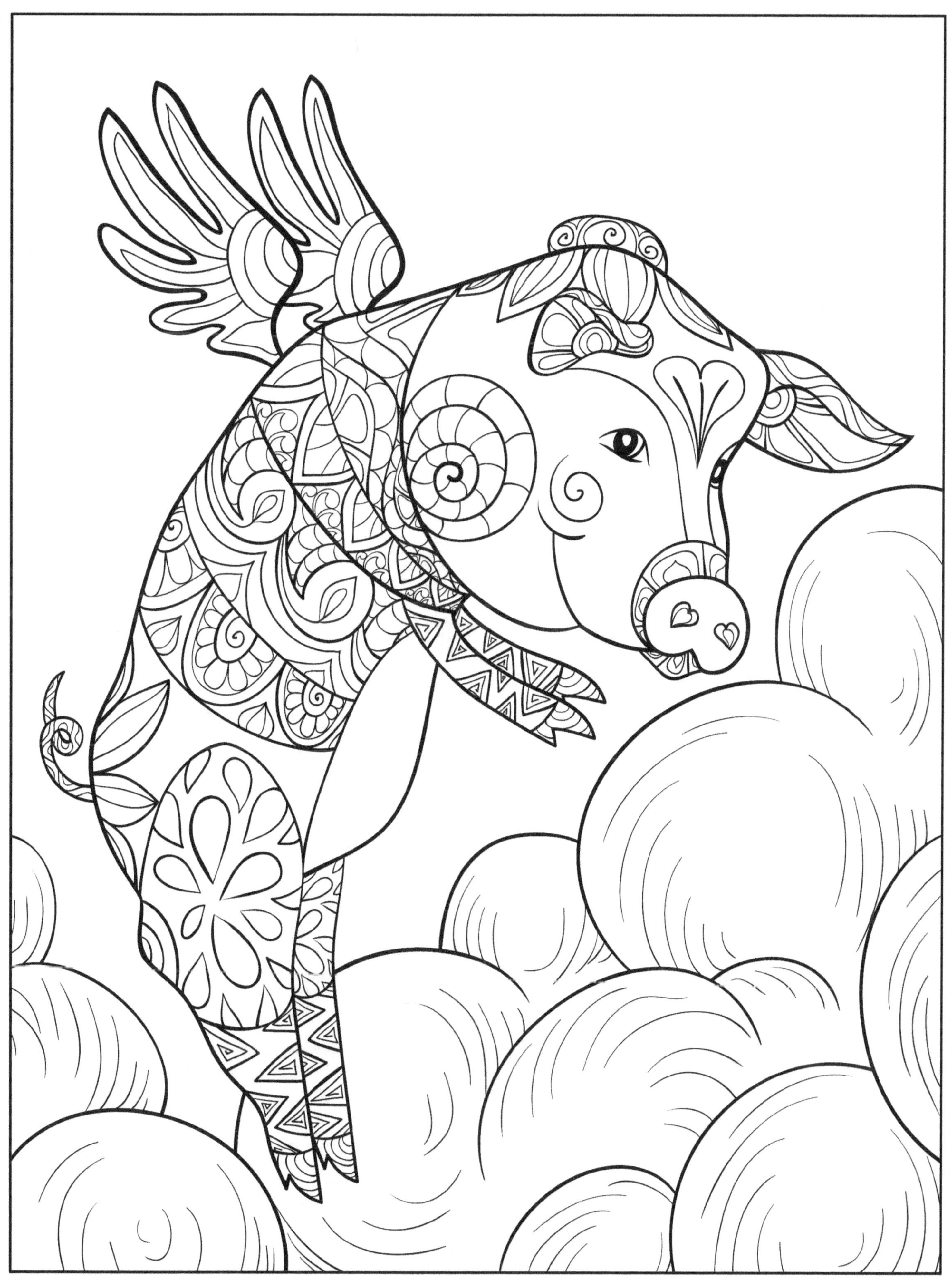

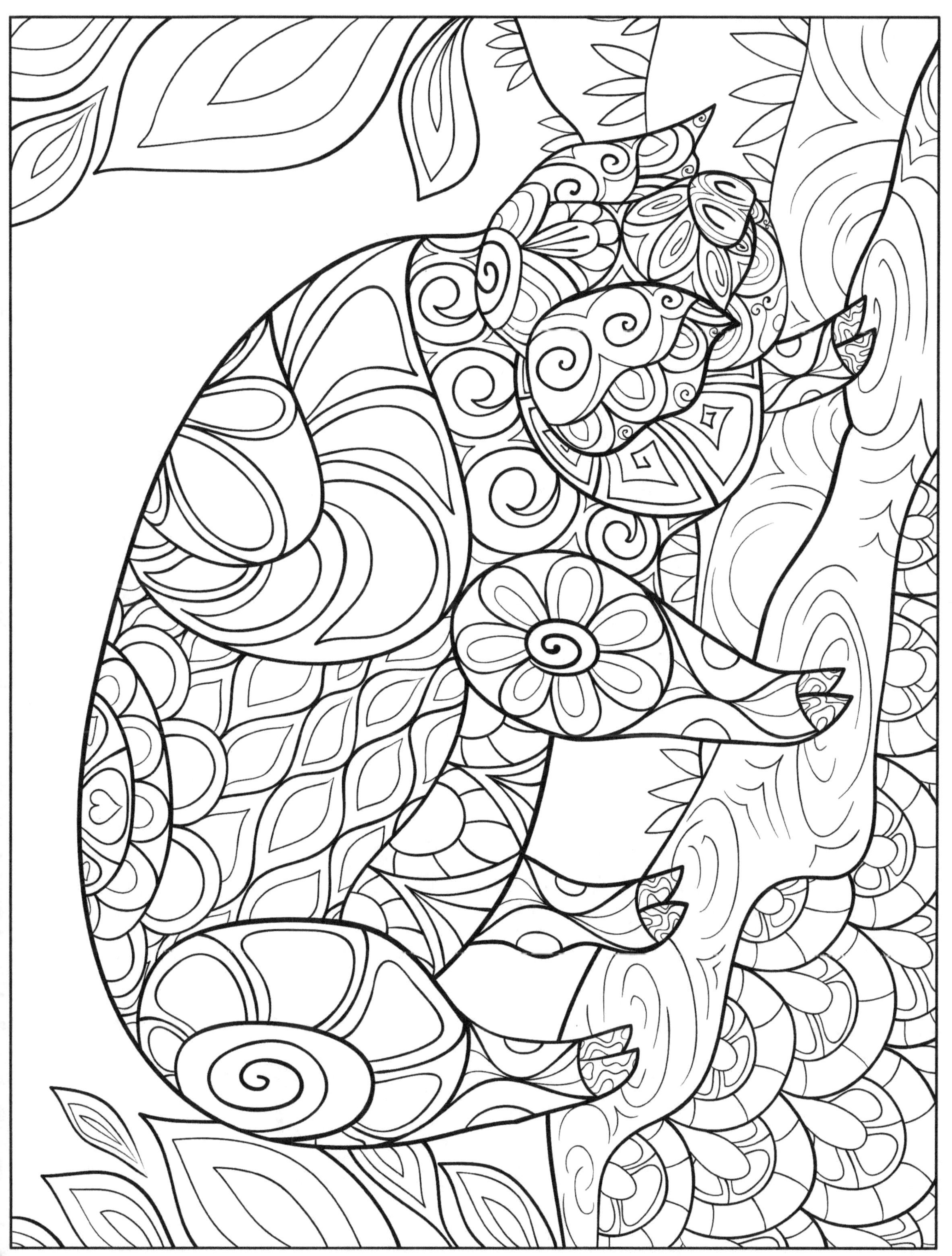

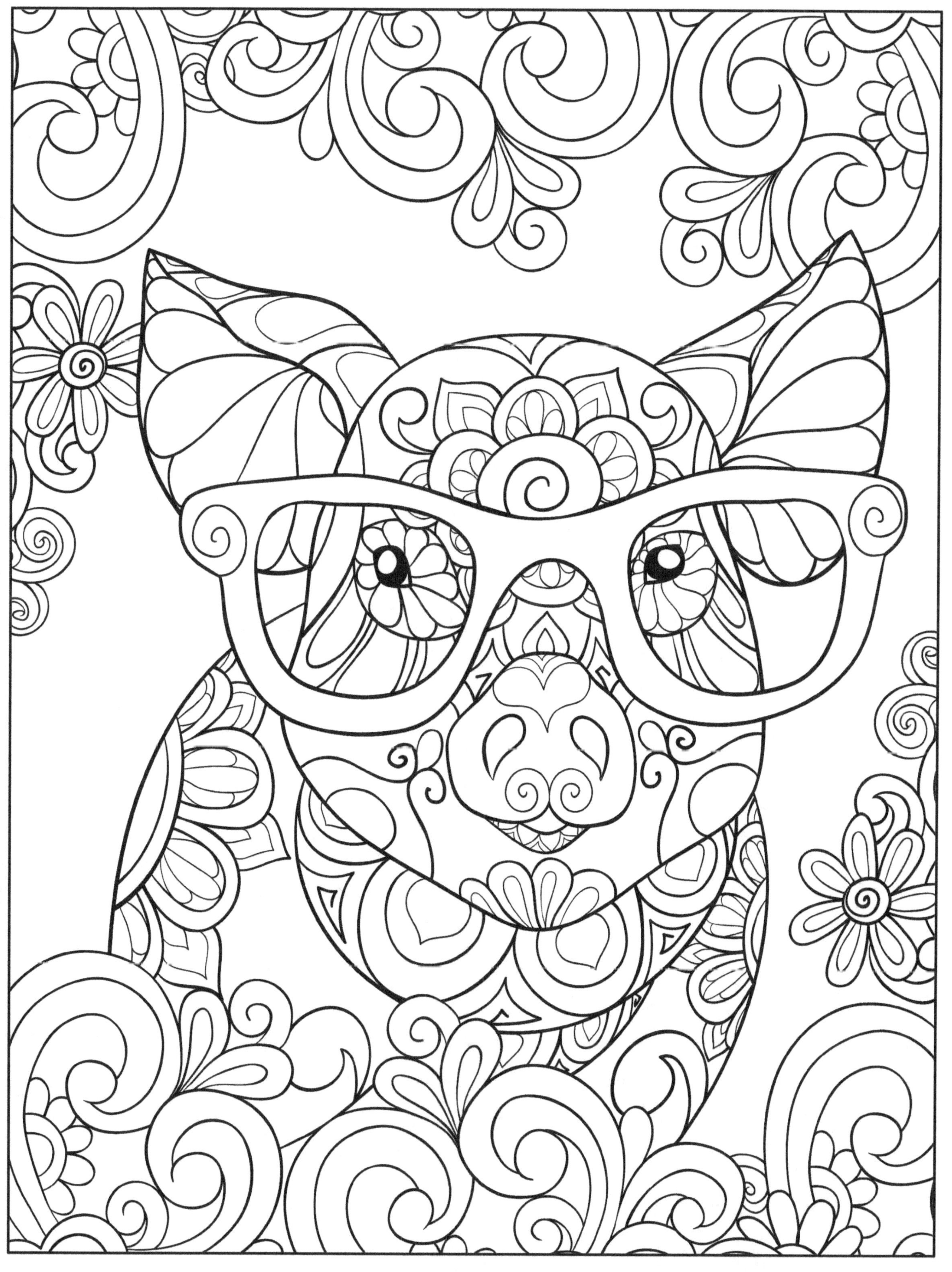

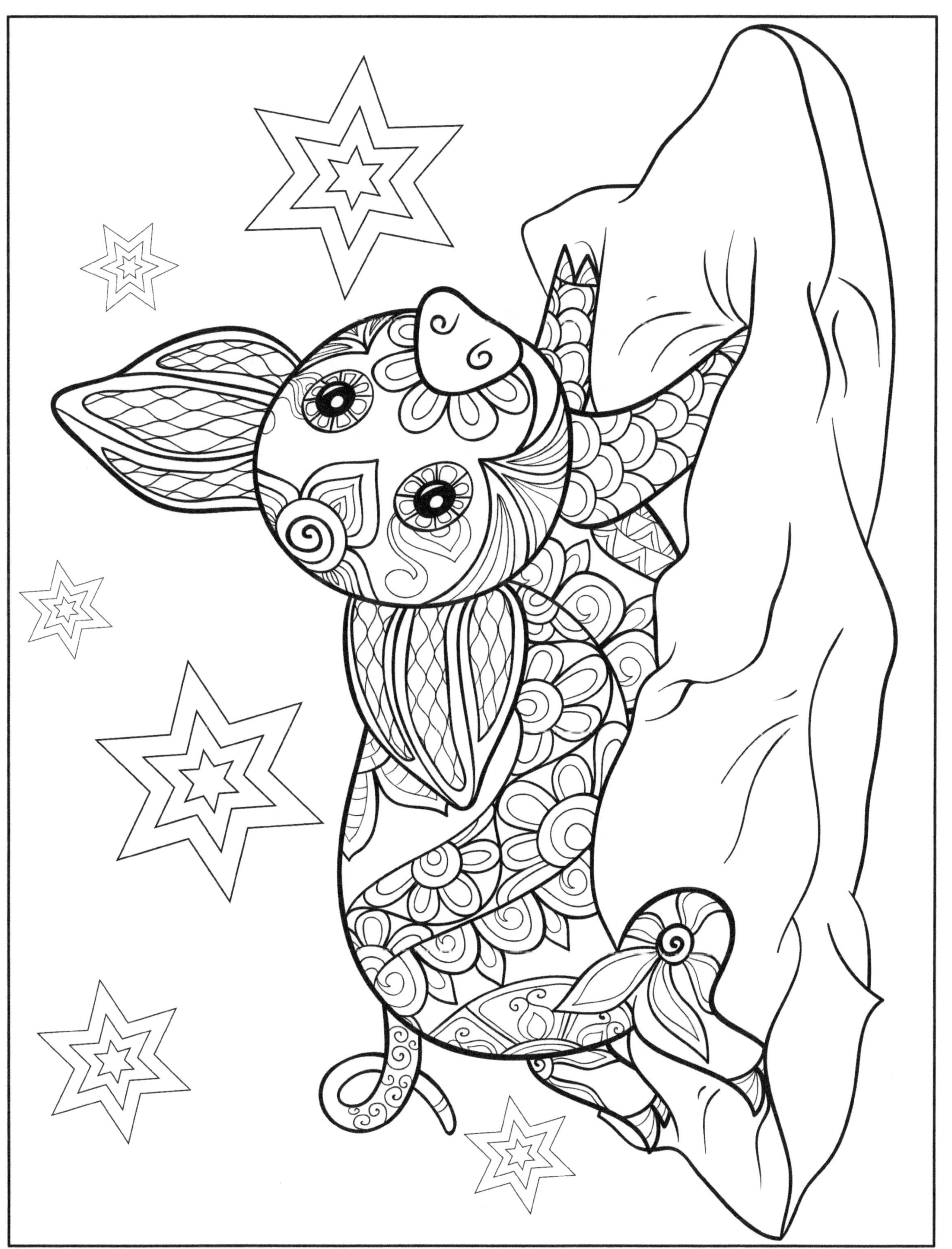

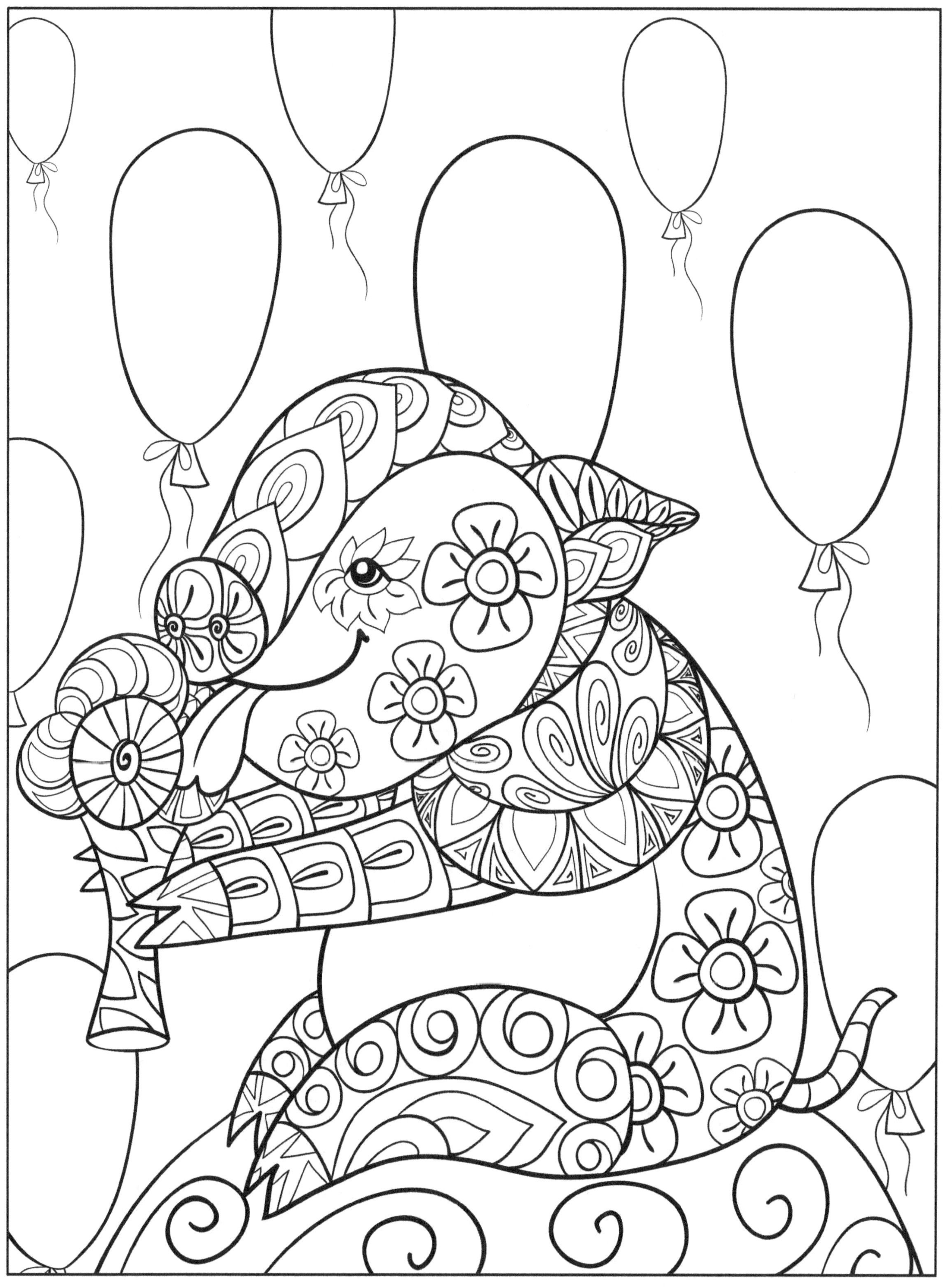

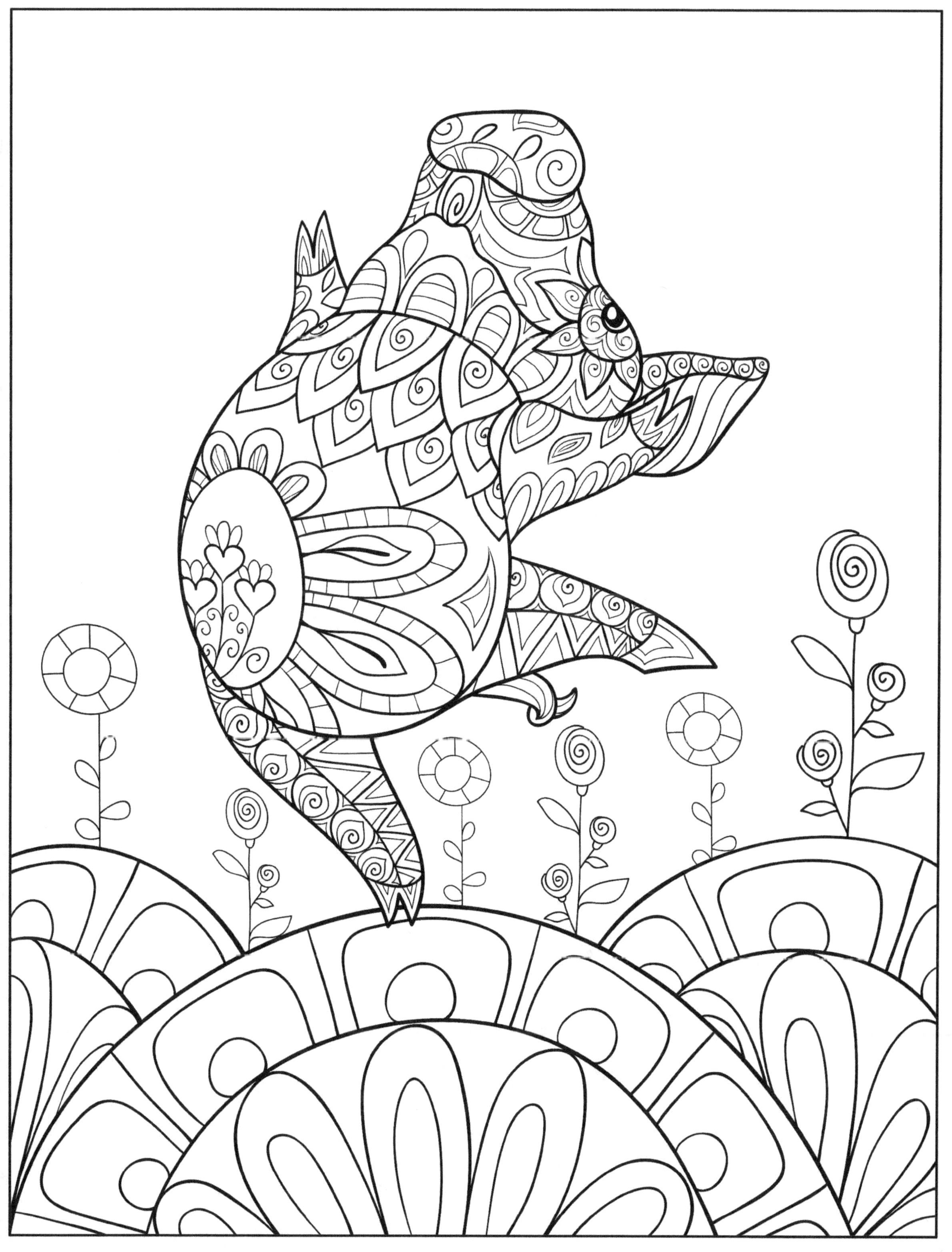

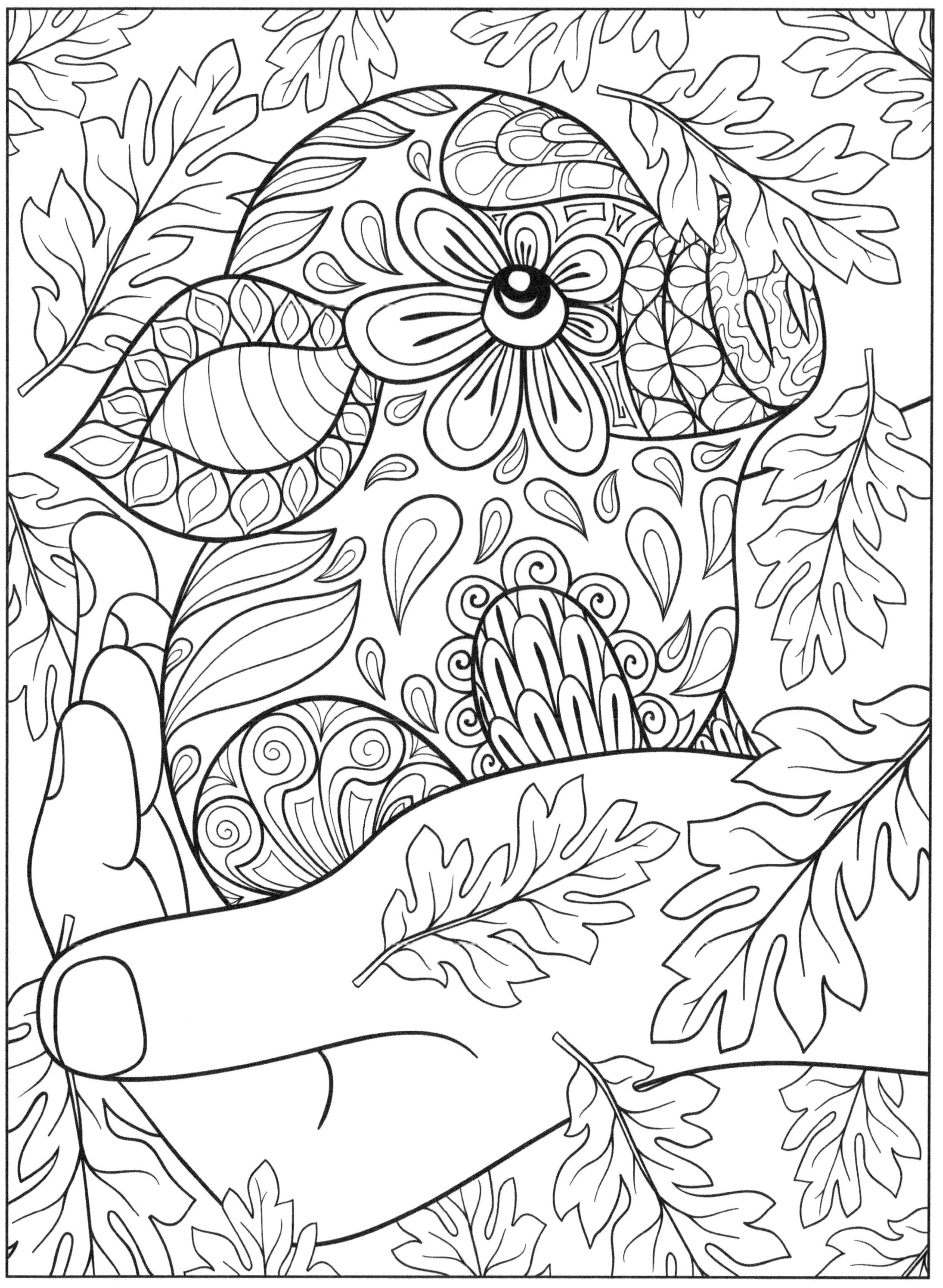

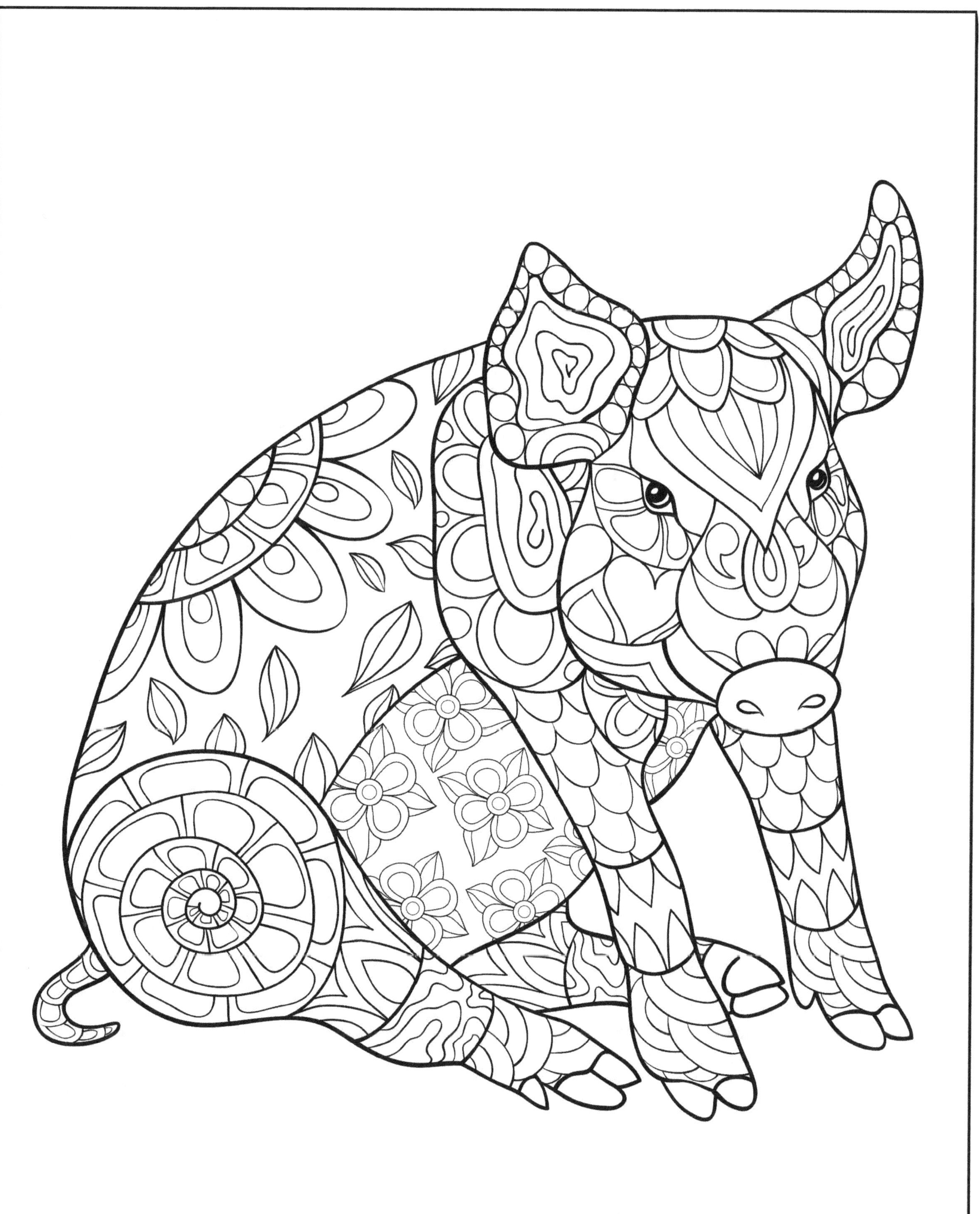

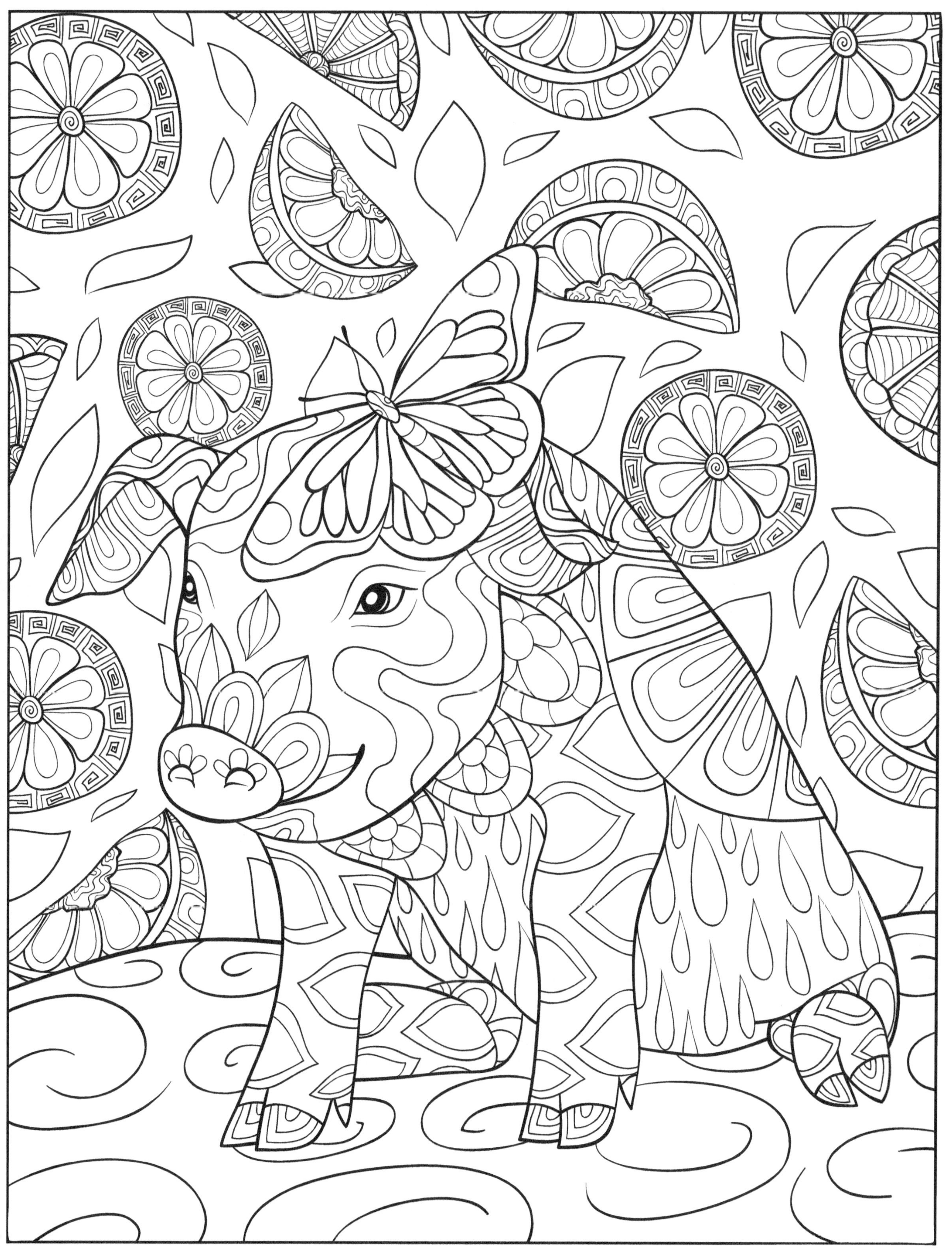

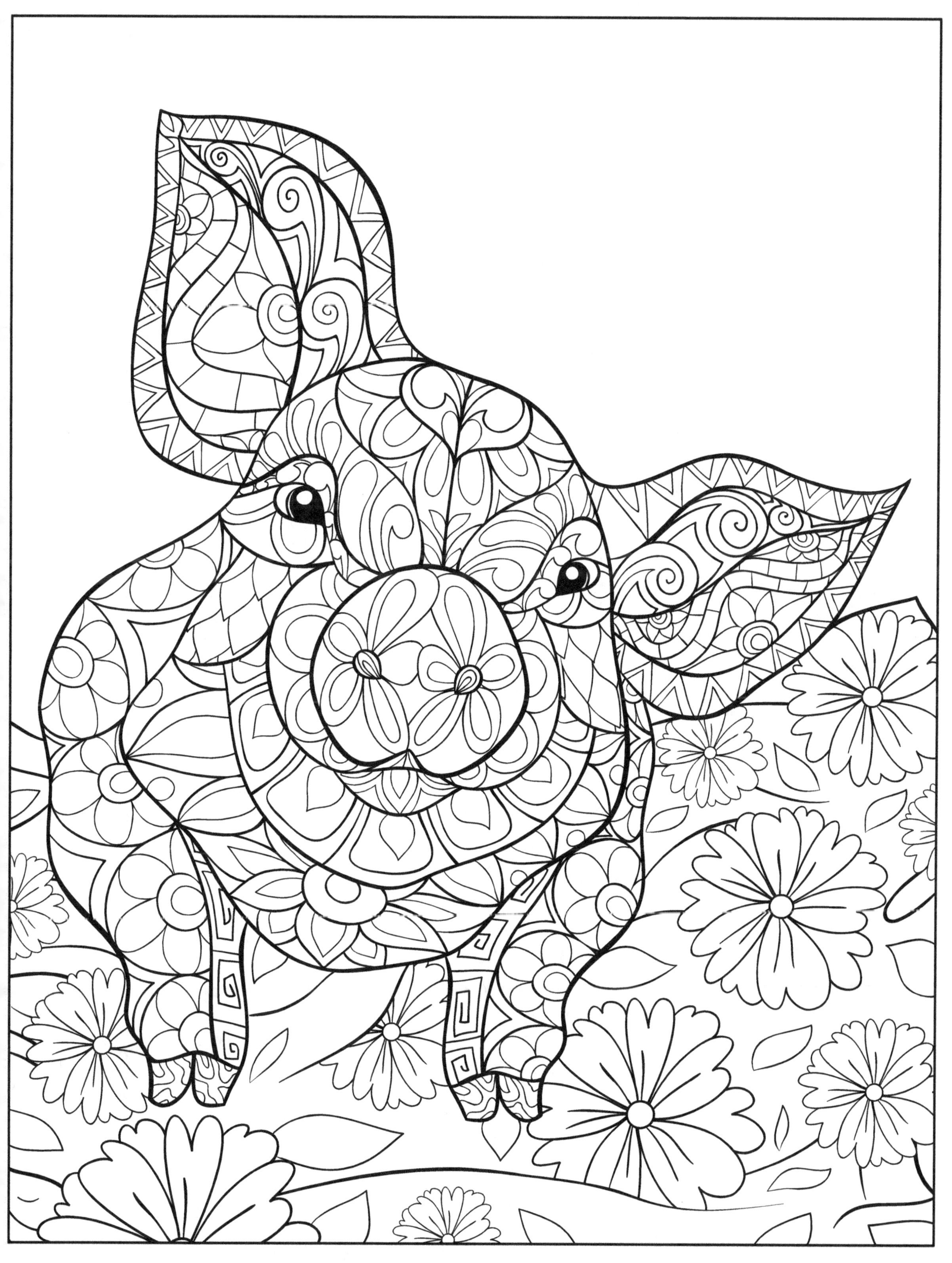

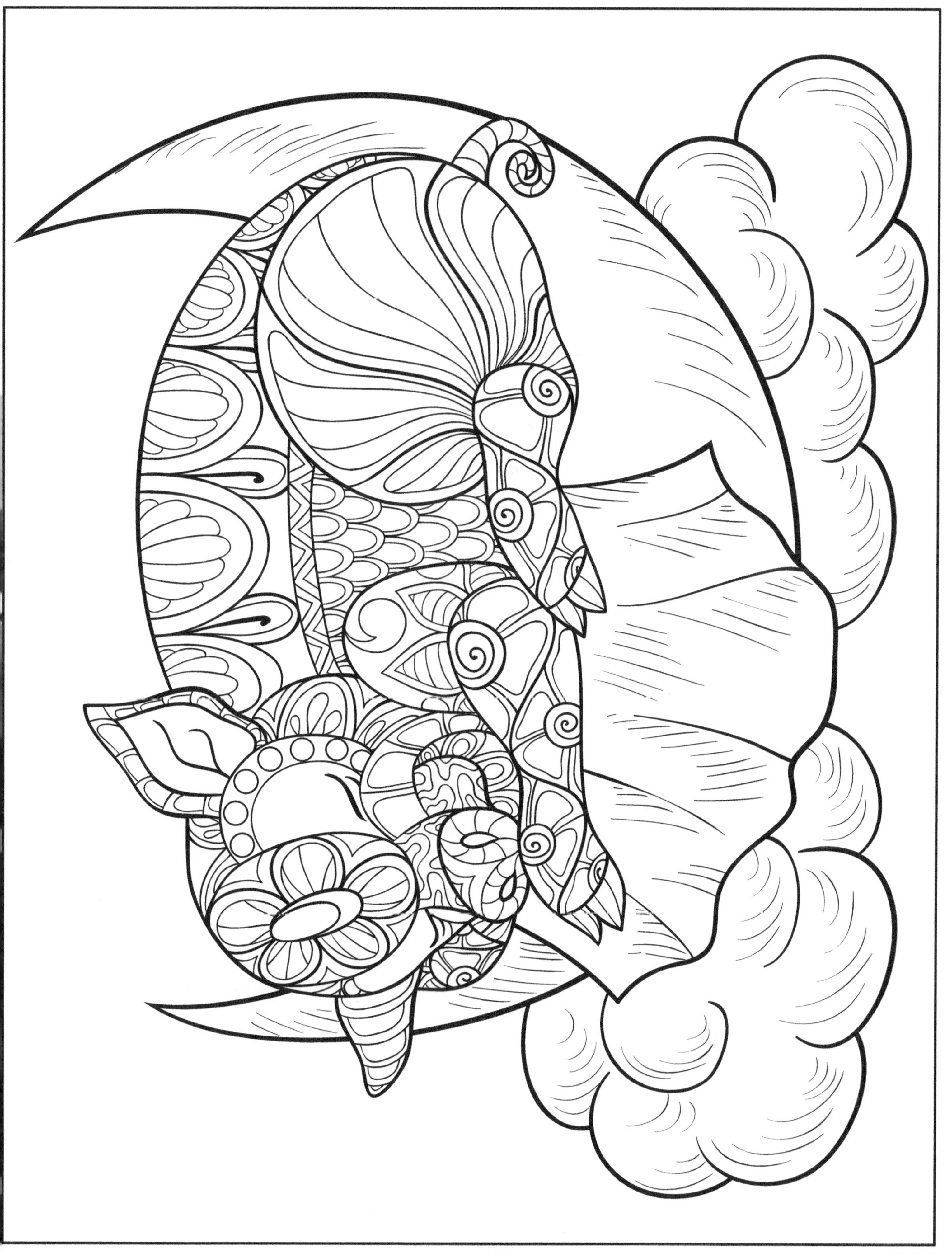

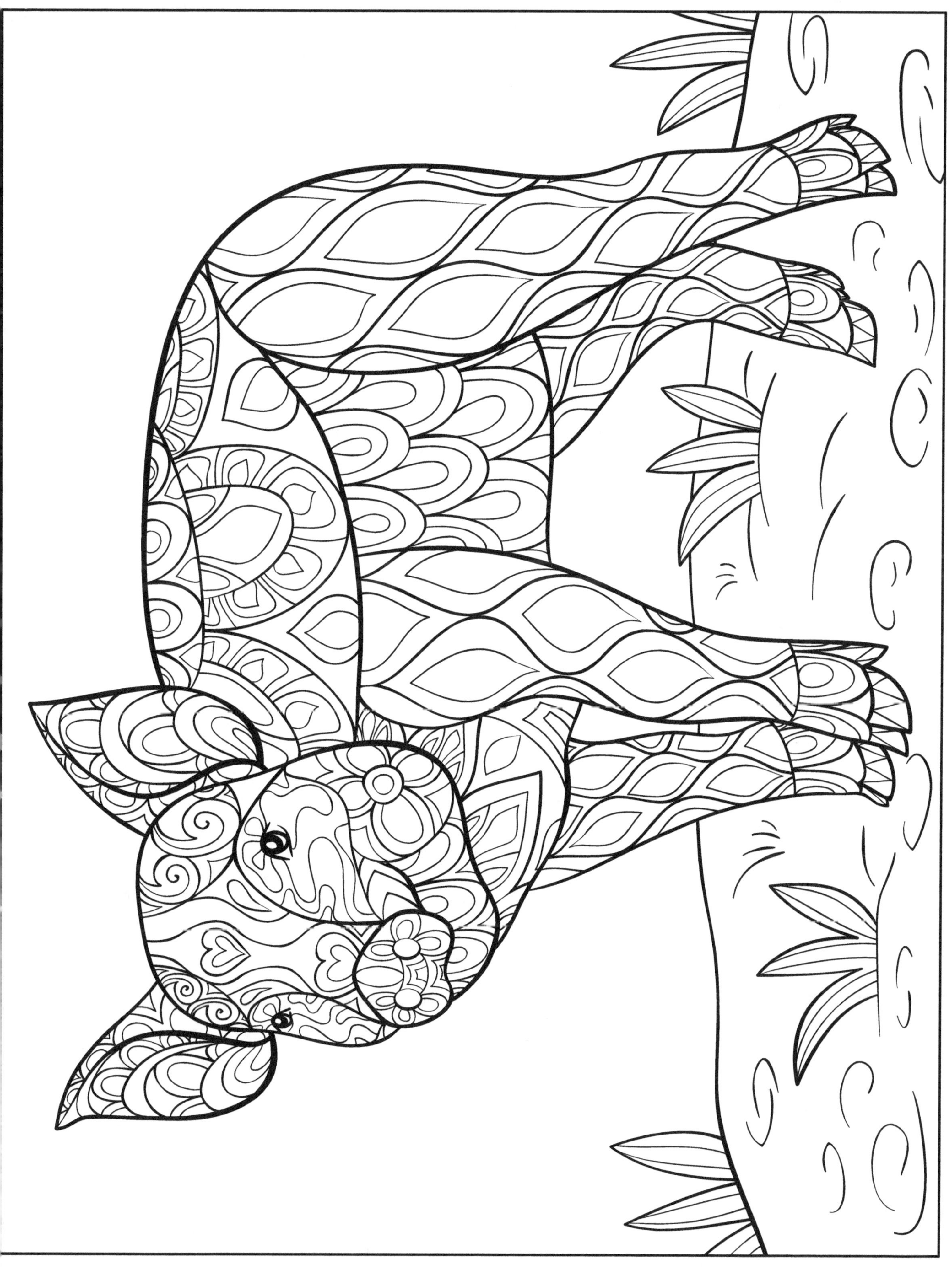

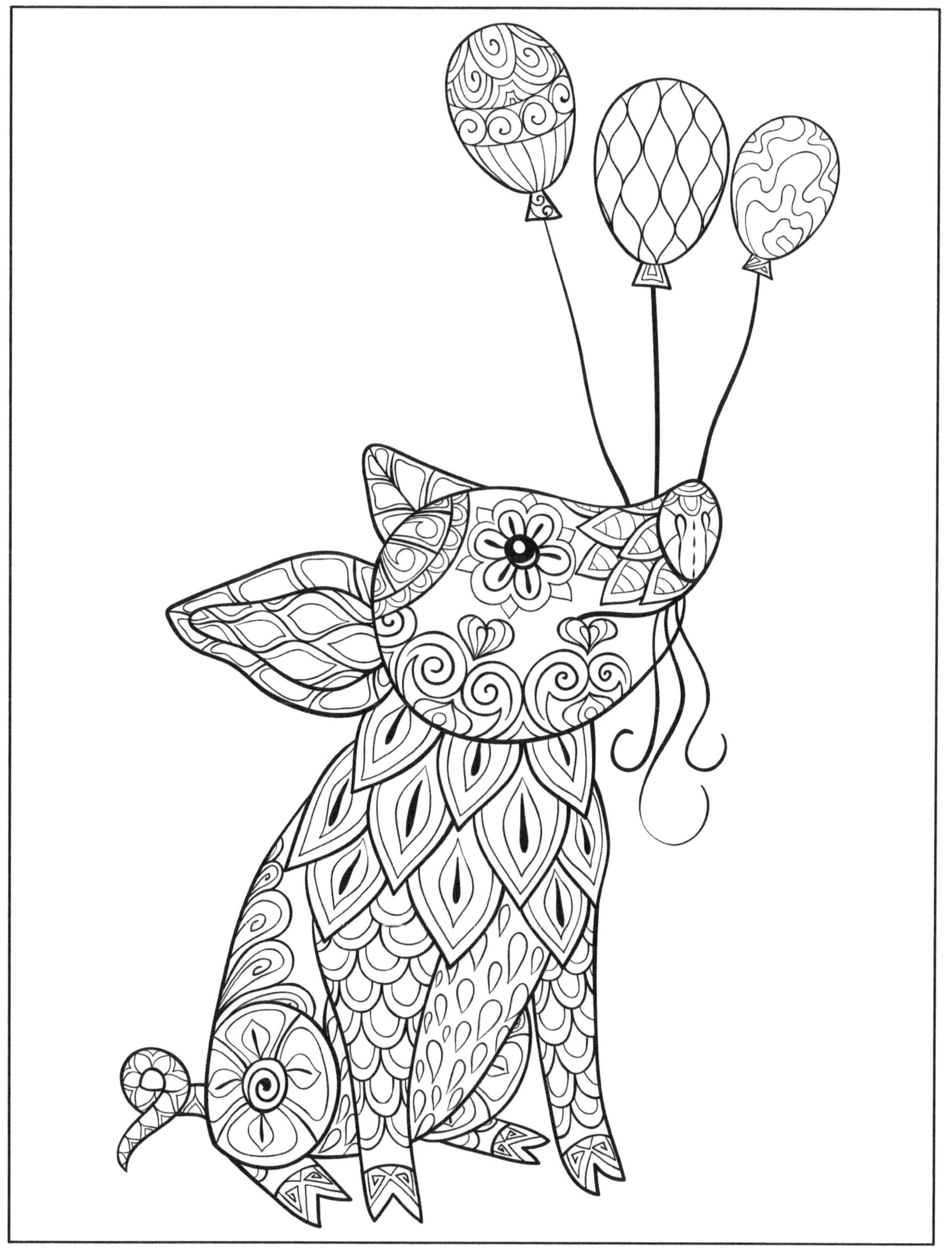

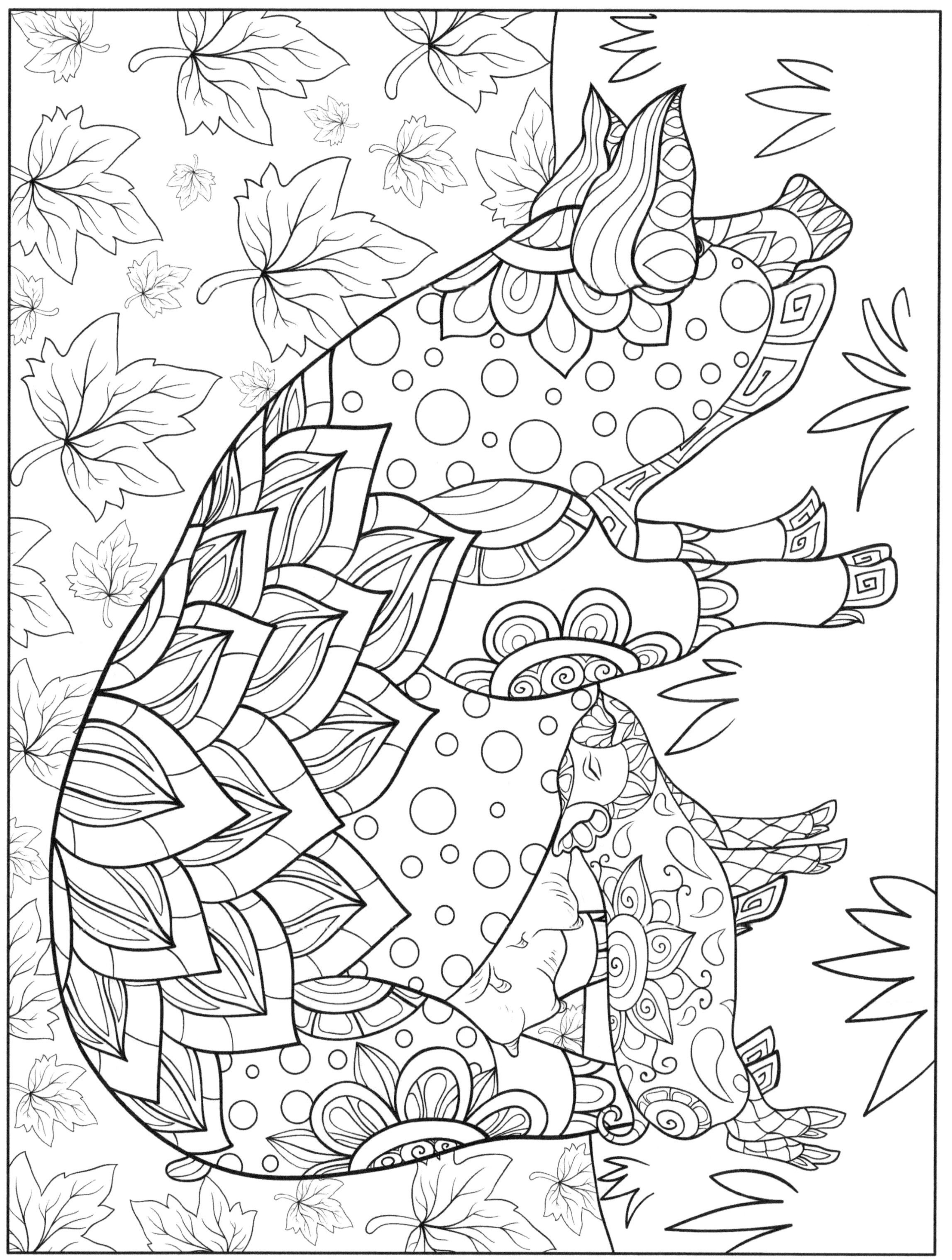

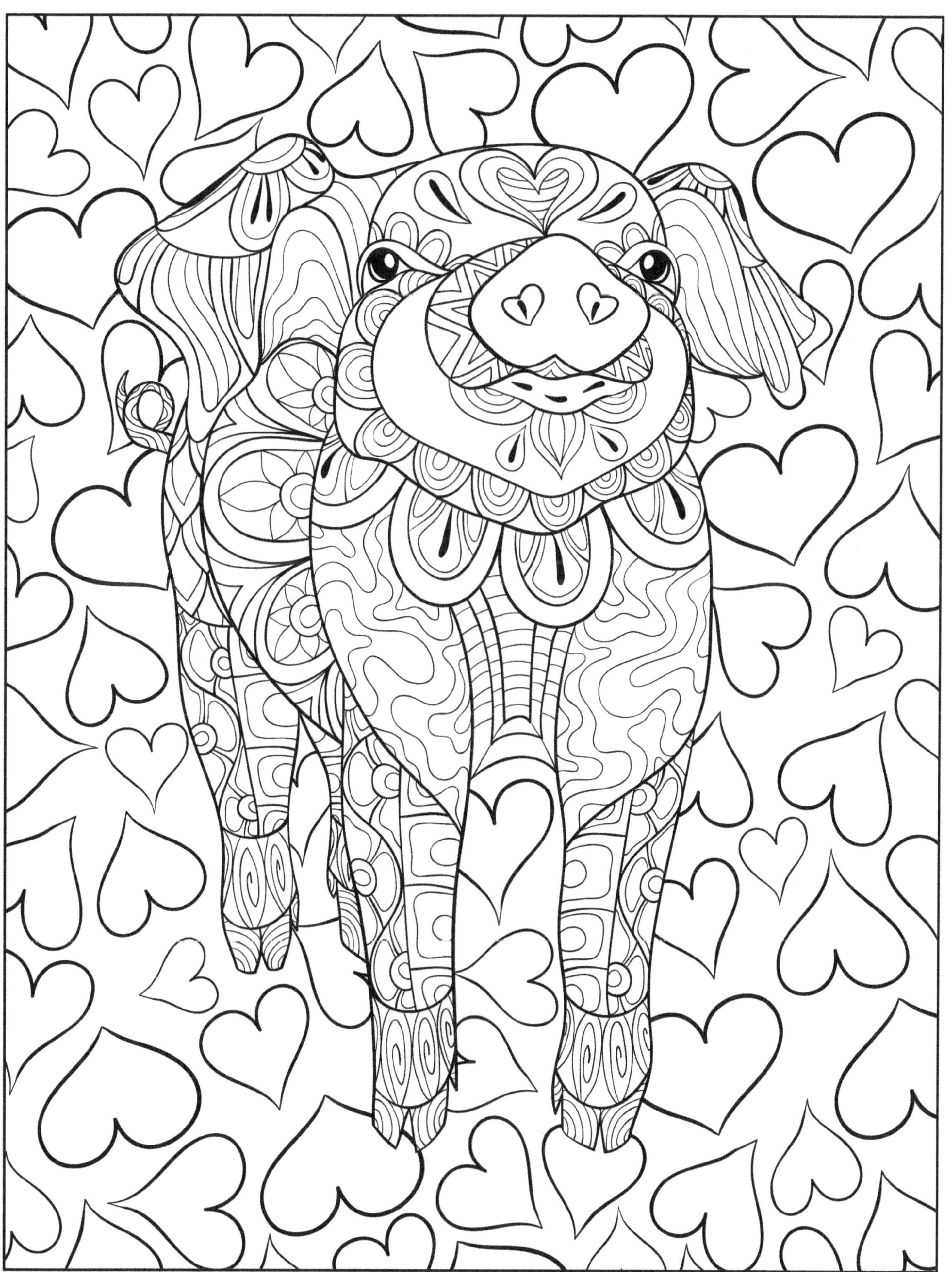

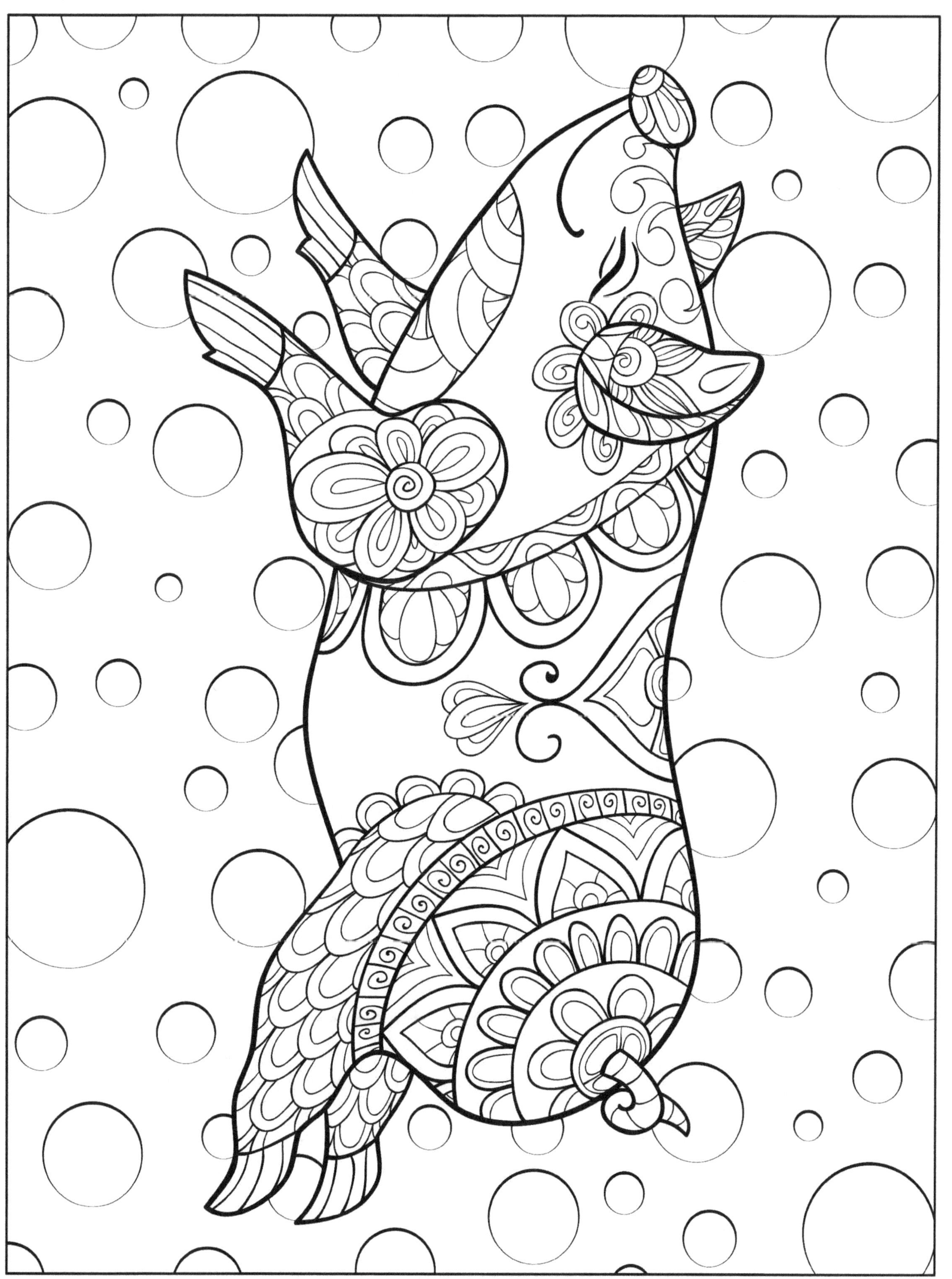

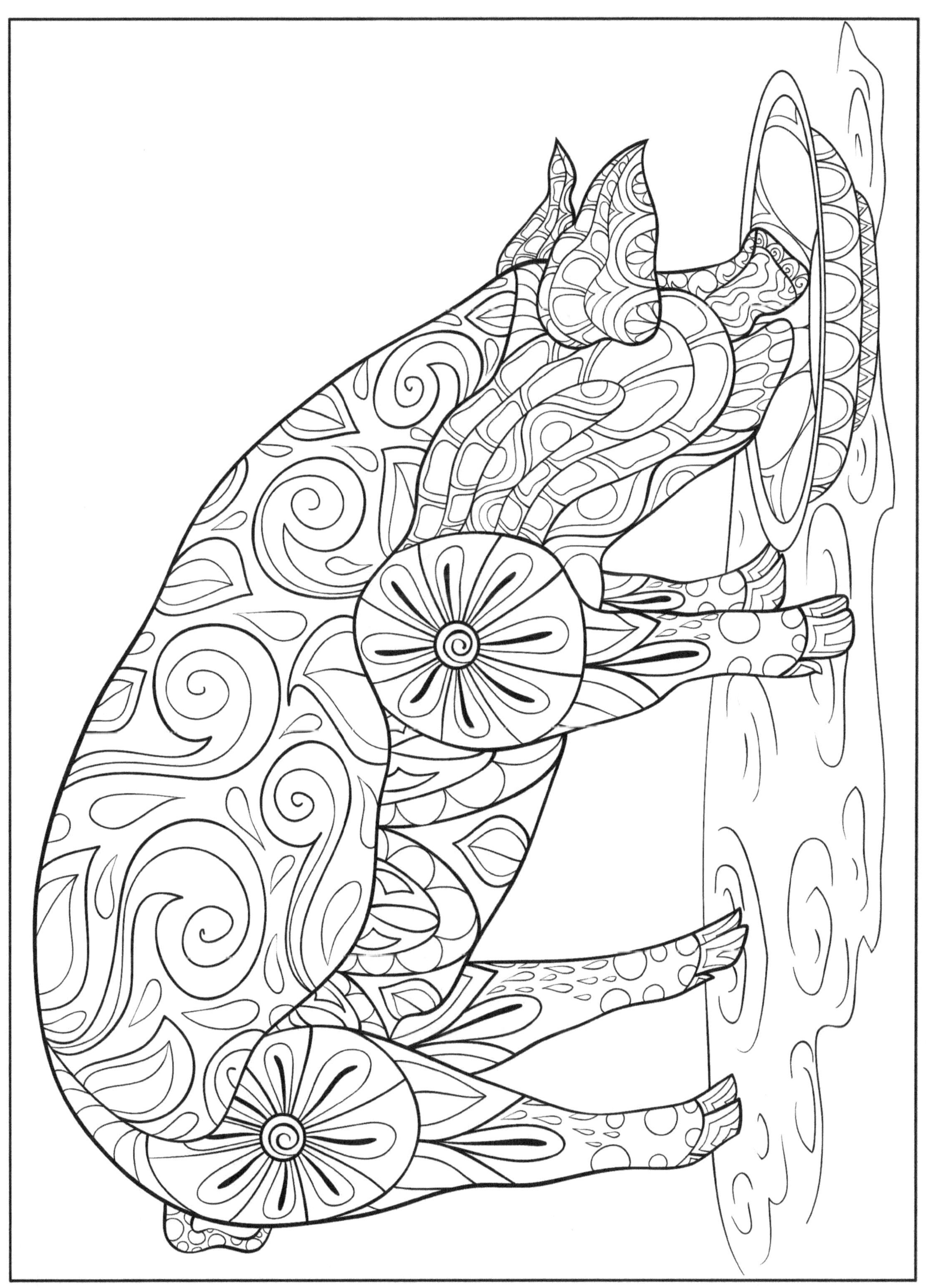

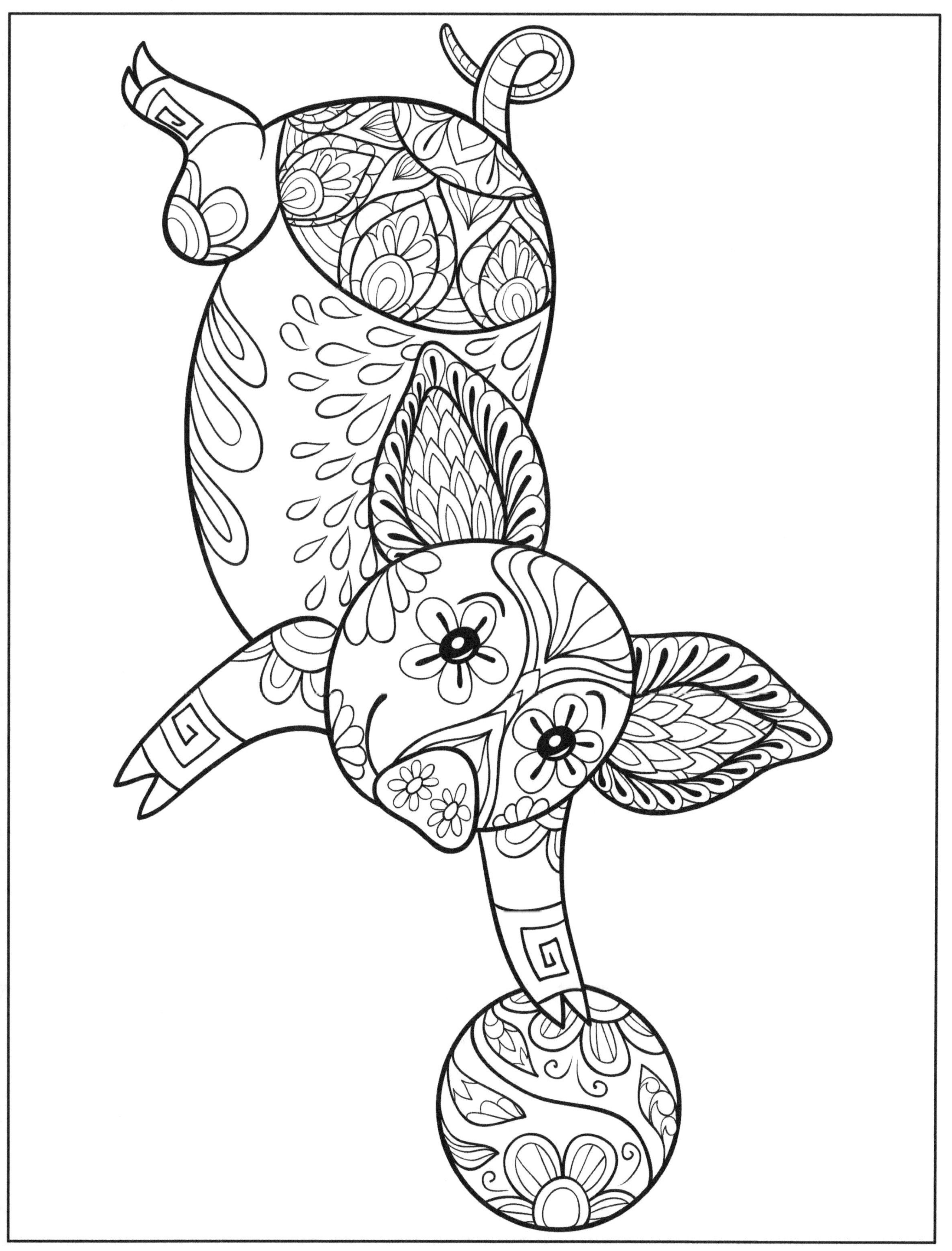

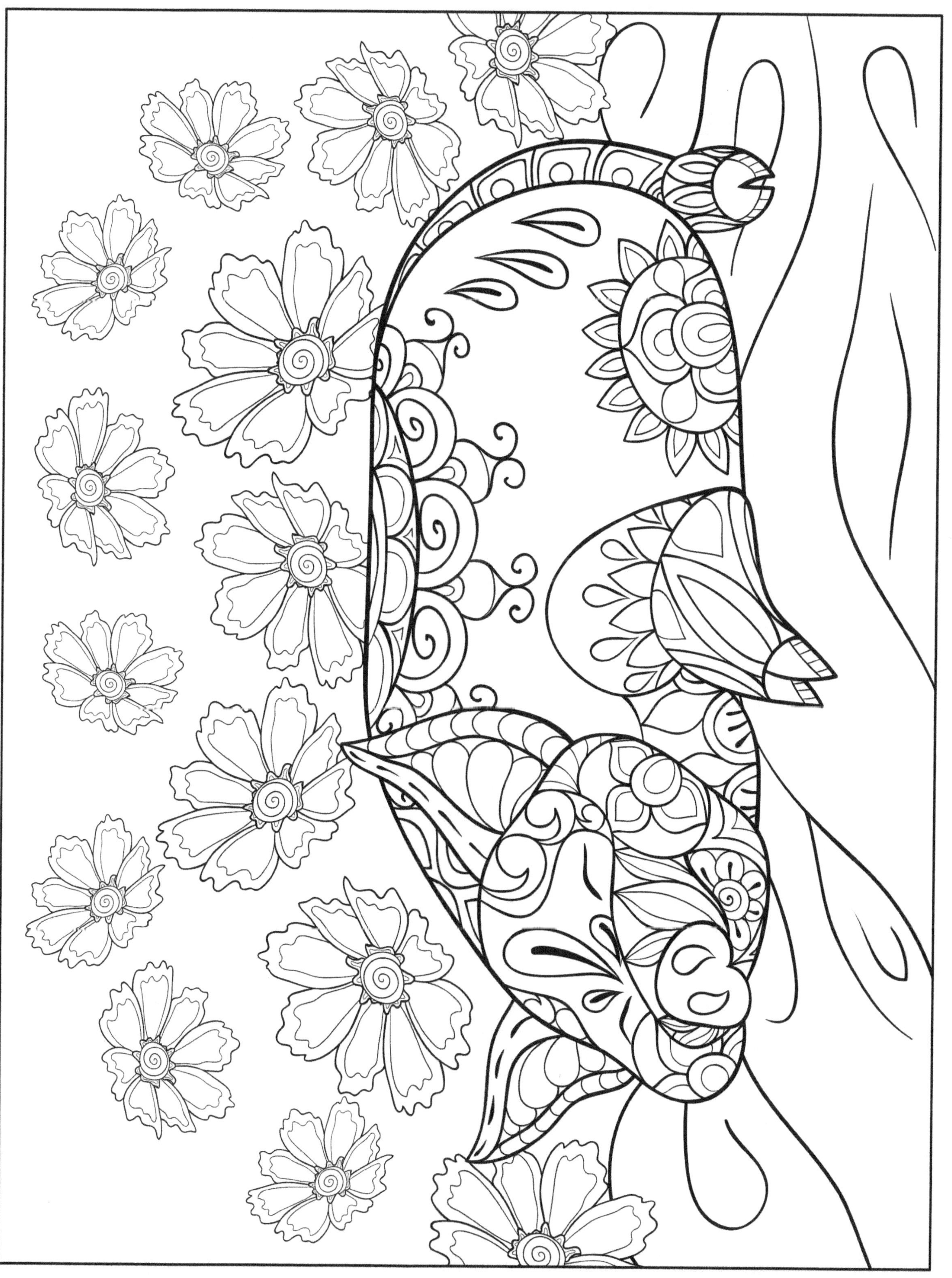

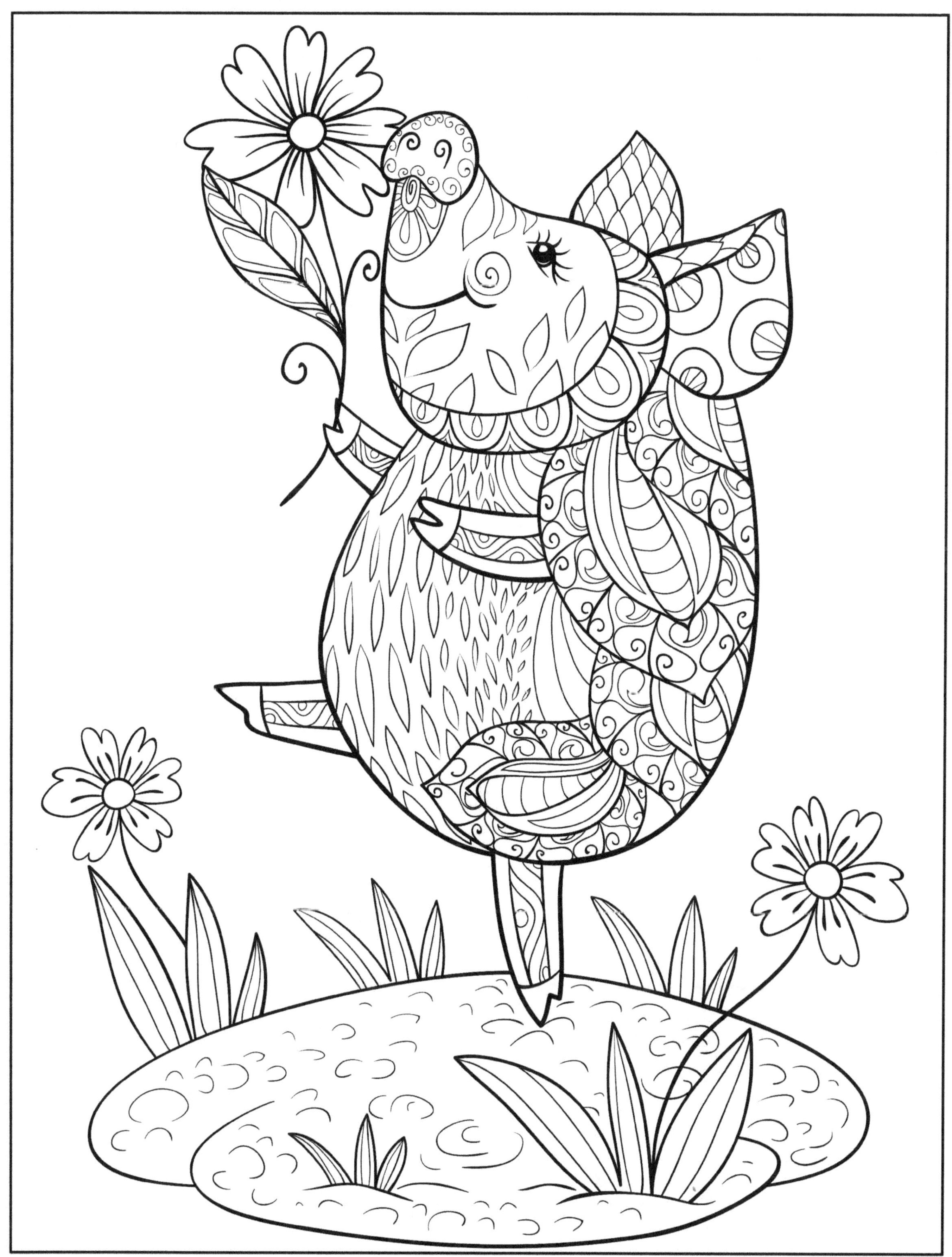

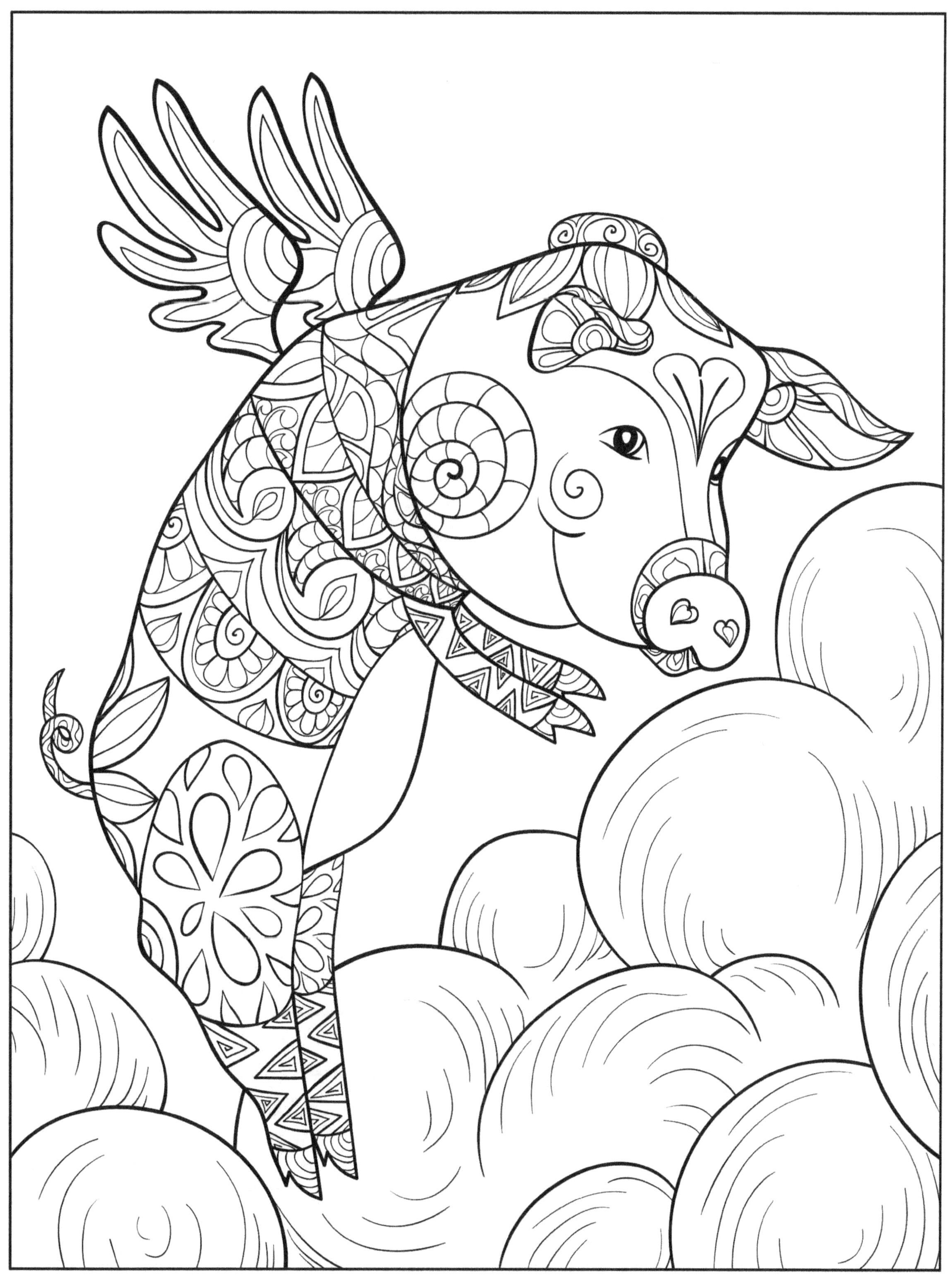

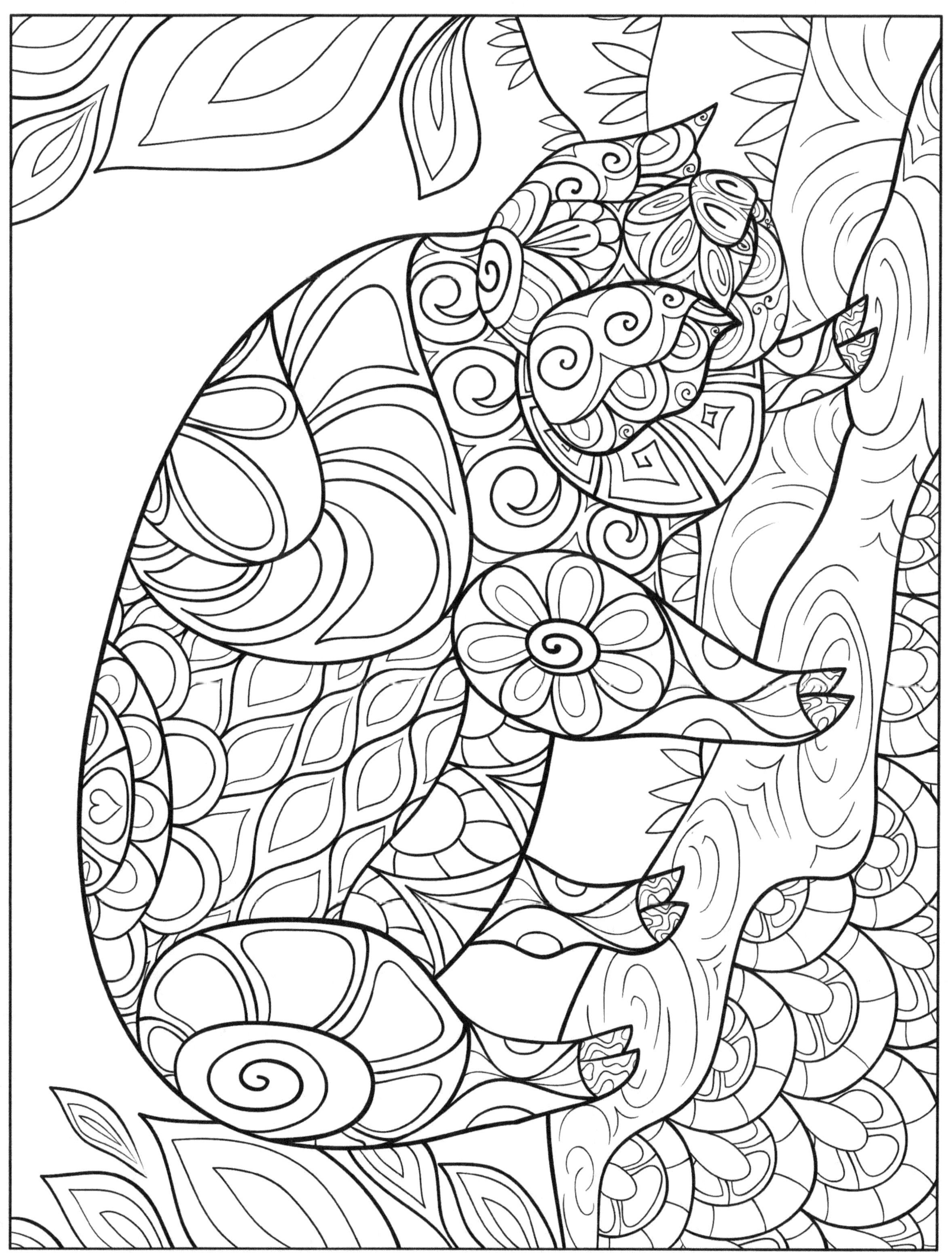

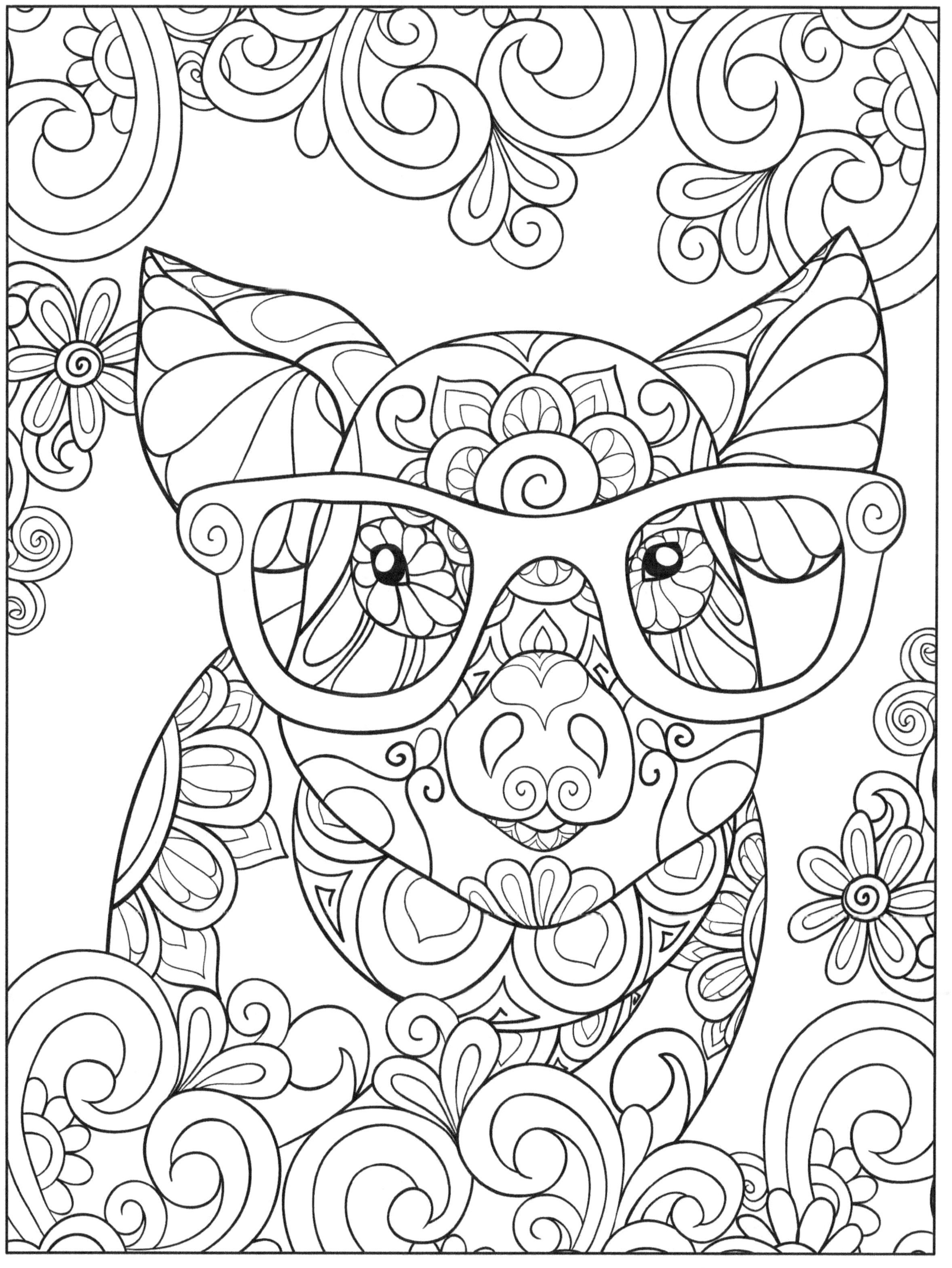

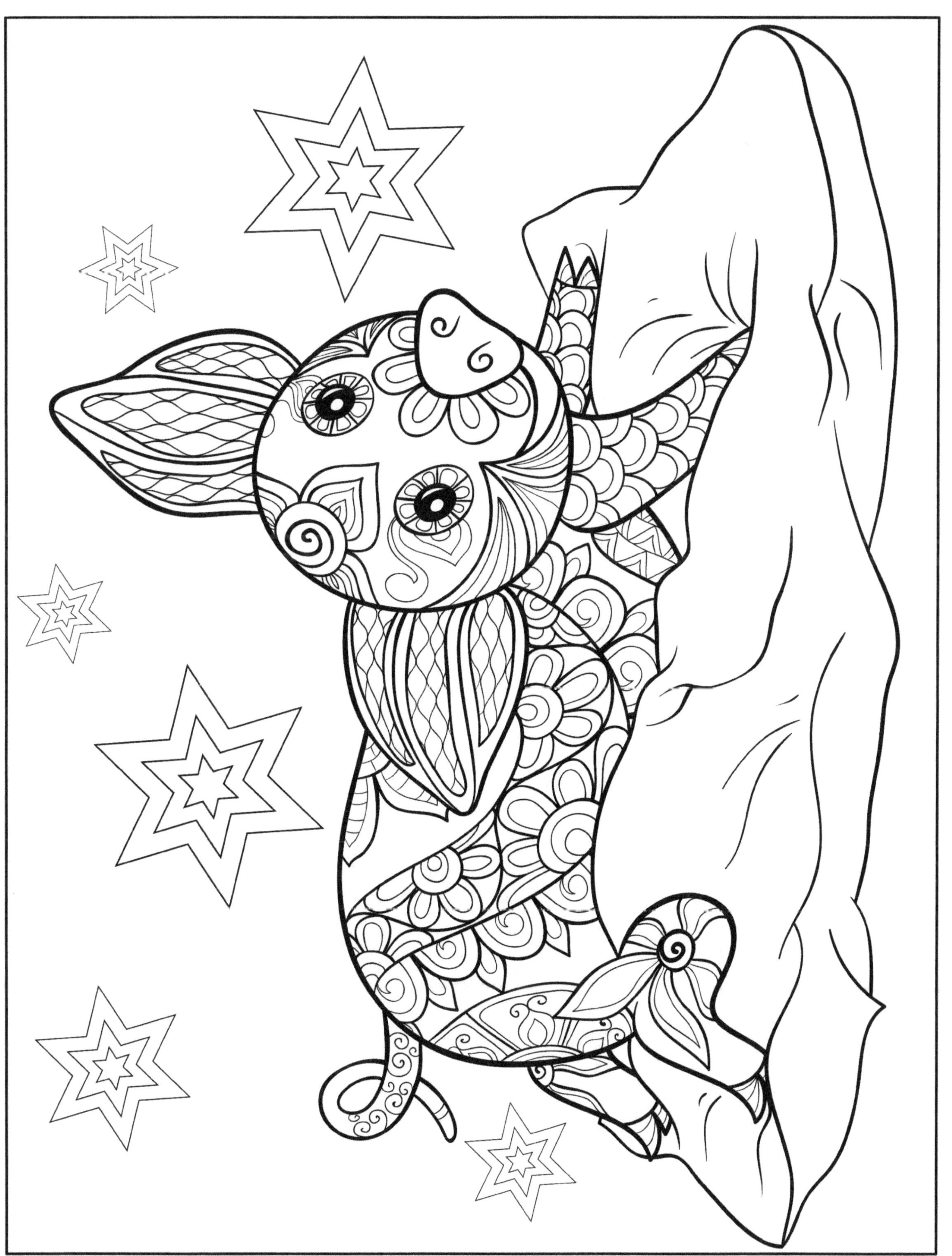

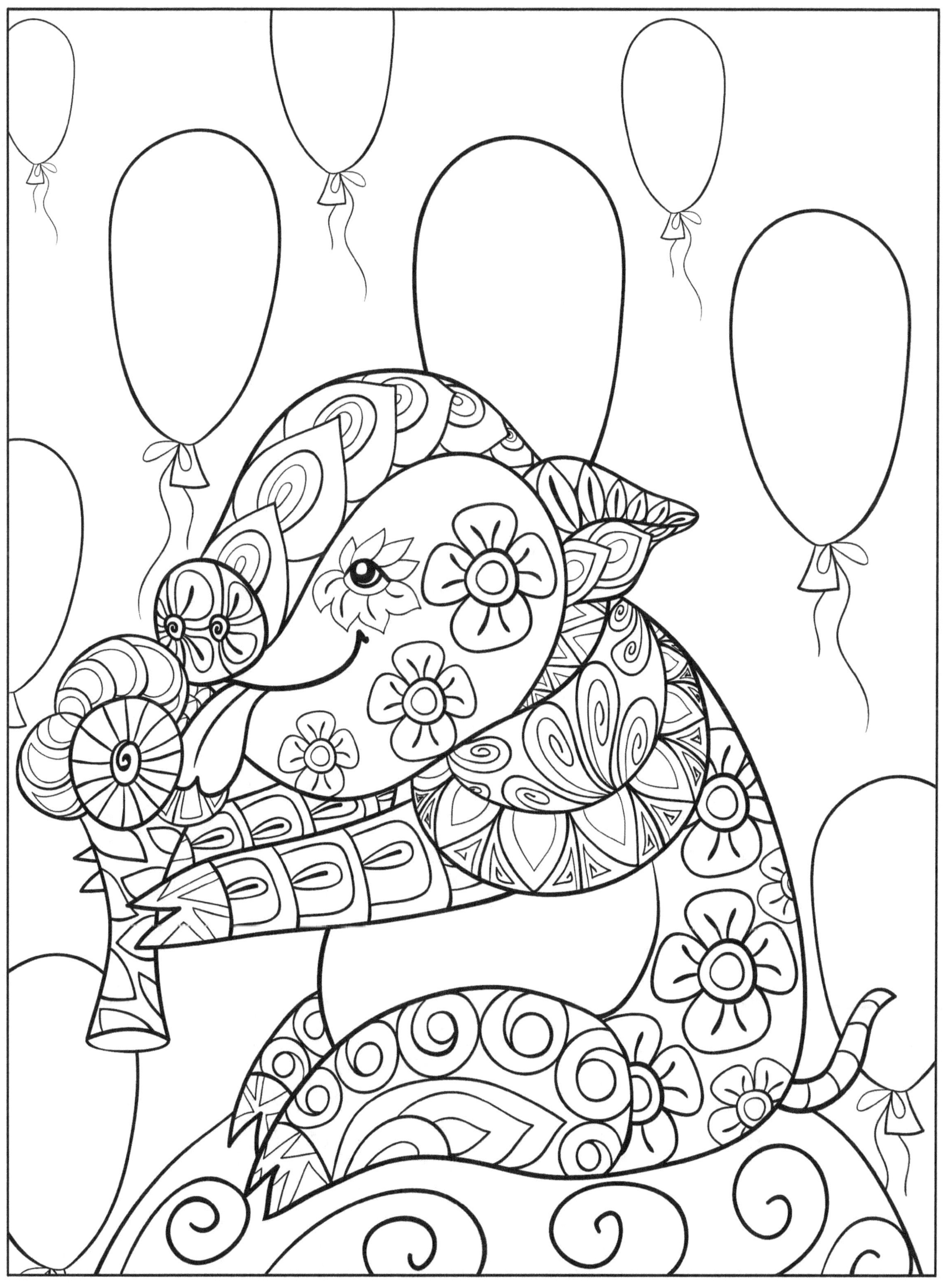

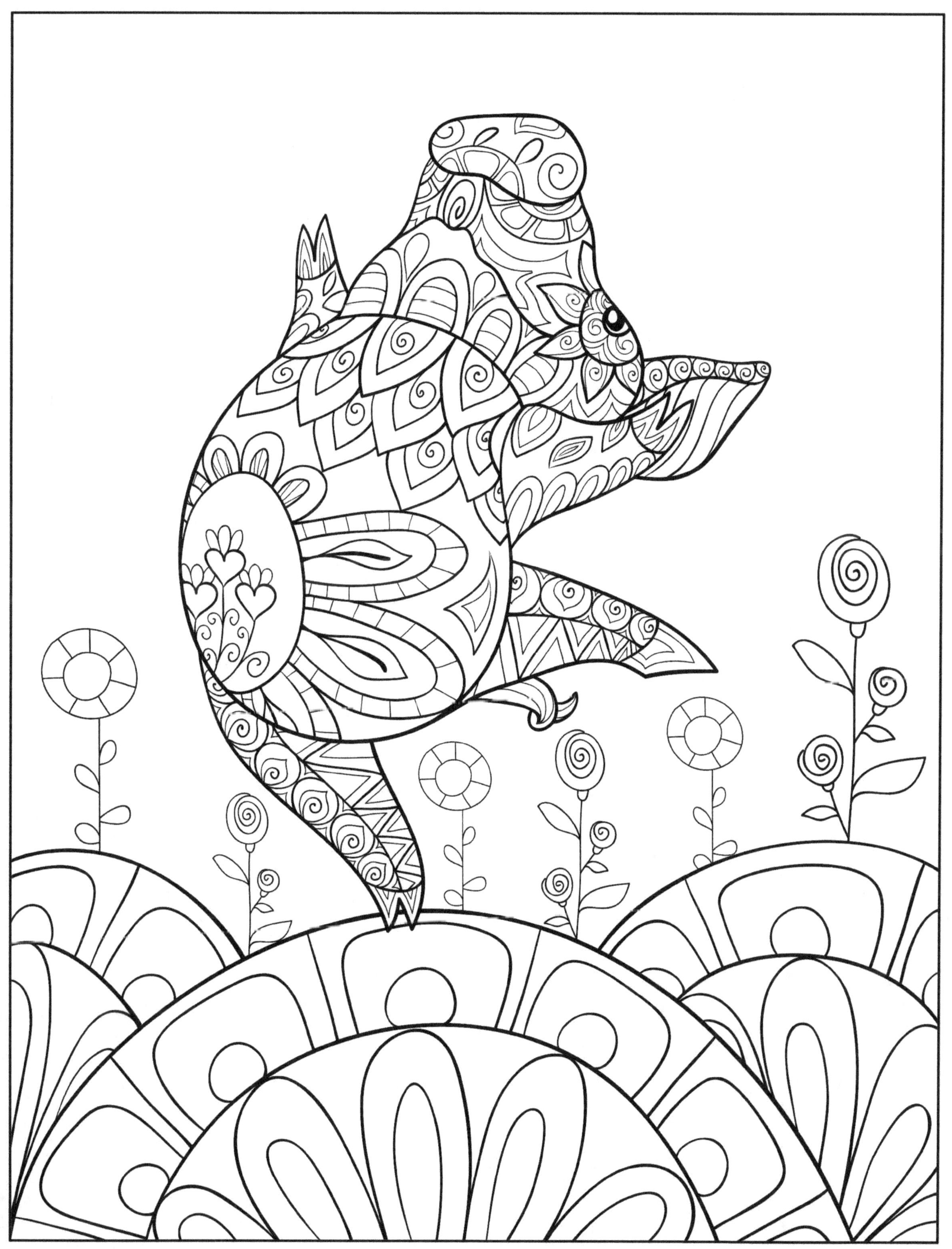

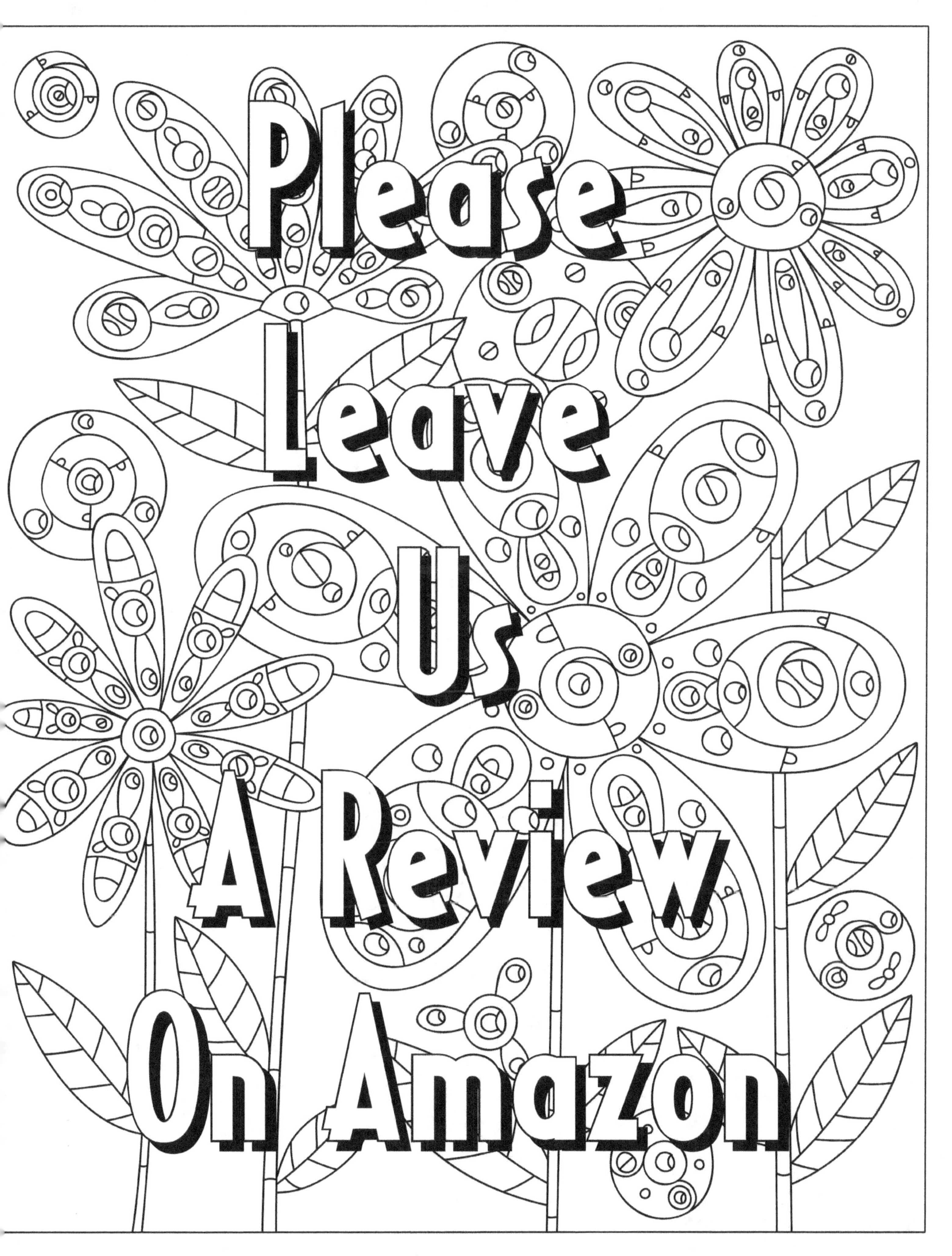

Please
Leave
Us
A Review
On Amazon

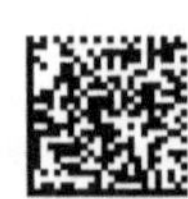

www.ingramcontent.com/pod-product-compliance
Lightning Source LLC
Chambersburg PA
CBHW080813280726
48660CB00018B/3329